PRAISE FOR
Receiving Healing from the Courts of Heaven

Jesus Christ healed them all, every time, everywhere He went (Matt. 12:15; 8:16; 14:36; 15:30, etc.). No one left His presence sick who called out to Him for healing. Father God always intended healing to be normal and sickness an aberration. Jesus called healing the children's bread because God always intended healing to be a natural, normal experience in everyone's life.

Just as the church has rediscovered the Spirit-filled life, the value of dreams and visions, and the five-fold ministries, so too has the body of Christ rediscovered the need for and the power in the ministry of healing. In these last days God has chosen to release His healing power in many ways. I have seen people healed in the hundreds of thousands and I know He can and does heal the sick through prayer cloths, anointing oil, dreams and visions, the laying on of hands, words of knowledge and faith, deliverance from demons, and the breaking of generational curses, just to name a few. I have also seen thousands healed during worship with no ministry at all. But now in these last days, God is once more pulling back the veil between Heaven and earth and releasing revelation on healing and its relationship to the Courts of Heaven.

Apostolic leader Robert Henderson has written a powerful book on healing from the perspective of the legal processes taking place in the courtrooms of Heaven. Satan, the Accuser of the brethren, uses every legal methodology in the Courts of Heaven he can to bring judgment on believers by appealing to God's own just nature. If satan can, he will use God's law to afflict God's people. Thankfully, God has raised up a group of spiritual pioneers of the heavenly way, and revealed to the church as a whole the inner workings of God's throne room and the Courts of Heaven, and Robert Henderson is one of these men.

In his book *Receiving Healing from the Courts of Heaven*, he shares many valuable insights to removing demonic attacks on the health of believers. I recommend you read this book carefully, digest it thoughtfully, and discover how to turn the legal processes of Heaven against the Accuser and gain your healing!

JOAN HUNTER
Healing Evangelist
Bestselling author of *Healing the Whole Man* and *Healing Starts Now*

The Holy Spirit raises up key voices at strategic times to release a word that helps to alter the course of church history. Robert Henderson is such a man, with such a voice and such a message. It is my joy to commend to you the life, ministry, and message of this sage man of God.

JAMES W. GOLL
Founder of God Encounters Ministries
International Best Selling Author
The Seer, The Discerner, The Lifestyle of a Watchman and others

Robert Henderson's book *Receiving Healing from the Courts of Heaven* is powerful and impacting. He skillfully and practically unpacks profound revelation from the Scripture regarding the believer's invitation into the Courts of Heaven to receive healing and freedom. You will love this faith-building book—I did!

Dr. Patricia King
Patricia King Ministries
www.patriciaking.com

Robert Henderson's teaching on the Courts of Heaven has been a revelation and key teaching for the Body of Christ. God has always had more to His covenant for us than we have taken hold of and functioned in our lives. In his new book, *Receiving Healing from the Courts of Heaven*, he gives scripture and life experiences to help us understand and apply this teaching. I encourage you to take back what Jesus, our Advocate, has provided and return sickness back to our accuser, satan, by receiving a judgment from God in the Heavenly Courtroom...in your behalf! We overcome by the Blood of the Lamb and the word of our testimony!

Dr. John Benefiel
Author of *Binding the Strongman Over America*
Presiding Apostle, Heartland Apostolic Prayer Network
Founder and Senior Pastor, Church on the Rock
Oklahoma City

The healing ministry of Jesus was such an essential aspect of His proclamation of the Kingdom of God, and is to be a significant aspect of it today as well. The Gospel makes provision for the whole person, spirit, soul, and body. The struggle for many who suffer is the age-old question as to whether it is the will of God to heal. Robert Henderson shares the same conviction that I do, that we are to believe God for healing for everyone who is infirmed. What Robert invites us to do in this new book is to learn how to ask and petition the Lord for healing, on the legal grounds of the promises of God that He made in the New Covenant. For those who have felt like they were going to cave in and fall short of seeing the hand of the Lord move on their behalf, *Receiving Healing from the Courts of Heaven* just might be the missing piece that will encourage your heart to petition, contend, and present your case before the Throne, and see God move on your behalf.

Dr. Mark J. Chironna
Mark Chironna Ministries
Church On The Living Edge
Longwood, Florida

RECEIVING HEALING

FROM THE

COURTS OF

HEAVEN

DESTINY IMAGE BOOKS BY ROBERT HENDERSON

Unlocking Destinies from the Courts of Heaven Curriculum

Unlocking Destinies from the Courts of Heaven

Operating in the Courts of Heaven

RECEIVING HEALING
FROM THE
COURTS OF
HEAVEN

REMOVING HINDRANCES THAT
DELAY OR DENY YOUR HEALING

ROBERT
HENDERSON

DESTINY IMAGE® PUBLISHERS, INC.

P.O. Box 310, Shippensburg, PA 17257-0310

"Promoting Inspired Lives."

This book and all other Destiny Image and Destiny Image Fiction books are available at Christian bookstores and distributors worldwide.

Cover design by: Eileen Rockwell
Interior design by Terry Clifton

For more information on foreign distributors, call 717-532-3040.

Reach us on the Internet: www.destinyimage.com.

ISBN 13 TP: 978-0-7684-1754-8
ISBN 13 eBook: 978-0-7684-1755-5
ISBN HC: 978-0-7684-1756-2
ISBN LP: 978-0-7684-1757-9

For Worldwide Distribution, Printed in the U.S.A.

3 4 5 6 7 8 / 22 21 20 19 18

CONTENTS

FOREWORD

I HAVE HAD THE PRIVILEGE OF KNOWING ROBERT Henderson for over 10 years. In this period of time I have gotten to know him very well. We have traveled together and labored side by side in many different facets of Kingdom ministry. It has been fascinating, as well as a great joy, to watch God expand his ministry, gifting and influence.

One of my first observations regarding Robert, and undoubtedly one of the reasons for his success, was his insatiable hunger for the Word of God. Not only would he read and study the Scriptures faithfully, but Robert loved to discuss different passages and texts with others. I soon realized he knew the Scriptures extremely well. His knowledge of God's word, in fact, is far beyond that of most leaders I have worked with. This hunger for truth has certainly not gone unrewarded; the Holy Spirit has and continues to honor it with great revelation. I don't believe I have ever heard Robert speak without learning something I did not yet know.

Another blessing for me has been to observe Robert's integrity. Sadly, the strength of some leaders' gifts is negated by the weakness of their character. I'm pleased to tell you this is not the case with Robert Henderson. I'm not acquainted with anyone who practices what they teach and preach more than this man. He is more than a friend of mine; he is an inspiration, modeling for me what it means to be a man after God's heart.

When Robert, in his first book, began receiving understanding of and sharing new language regarding the throne room of heaven—referring to it as the court(s) of heaven—I was fascinated. I knew satan often attacked us based on legal ground given to him, but the revelation with which Robert taught this opened much new understanding for me and many others. This teaching, of course, has now impacted hundreds of thousands of people around the world.

It has come as no surprise for those who know him that Robert is now linking this teaching to the subject of divine healing. For many years, he has been used greatly in this area of ministry, praying for many people who have been healed. It has, in fact, been one of his passions. While observing him pray for people, however, what stood out to me was the intensity of his desire. I have seen many, many people pray for sick and suffering individuals. I don't believe, however, that I have ever seen anyone do so with more passion and determination to see the suffering individual healed. It seemed at times that he was "attacking" the sickness with his prayers. His anger toward the infirmity and desire to see the person healed was both stunning and refreshing. He truly embodied the phrase "moved with compassion."

That same passion comes through the pages of this book. It is obvious when reading it that the words are coming from one who is desperate in his desire to see people healed. You'll sense that passion...and reap the rewards.

Also, the revelation I have heard emanating from Robert on so many occasions flows from this book. You will read statements you have not heard before, and will be motivated to think deeply about them. Ask the Holy Spirit to open your understanding and teach you His ways. You'll learn much as you read these insights. As you apply them, healing will manifest.

I wholeheartedly join my faith and prayers with Robert's— that many people will find their healing through the application of the truths in these pages. Our sincere desire is that you find your breakthrough of healing through the suffering, sacrifice, and provision of our divine healer, Jesus Christ, to whom belongs all the glory.

Sincerely,
DUTCH SHEETS
Dutch Sheets Ministries
Bestselling author of *Intercessory Prayer,*
Authority in Prayer and *An Appeal to Heaven*

INTRODUCTION

I AM ONE WHO HAS FUNCTIONED IN THE MINISTRY OF healing for many years. I have partnered with and seen the exhilaration of people as they are delivered from disease. There is nothing more joyful for me than this. However, I am very aware of the pain, disappointment, and trauma of people believing for healing without it ever coming. I have watched people's suffering continue for years while they diligently believed for their miracle. I have witnessed those who "died in faith," believing to their very last breath that they had been healed and their lives lengthened. I have watched what appeared to be a measure of healing come, only to see it vanish and sickness and disease return.

In the midst of all this, I have seen well-meaning people and ministers try to bring comfort and understanding in these situations. Some, in my estimation, are outright cruel. They imply or even clearly state that it is a lack of faith on the sick person's part that is denying their healing. So now the person not only is suffering with sickness and pain, but they feel condemned as well. Even though I believe that faith is essential to healing, I believe it is fruitless to chide someone with this reasoning. In fact, those ministering to the sick can use their own faith to see people healed. The ones healed will have to develop a faith to "hold" their healing, but the initial experience of healing can be secured through those praying. We will investigate this later in this book.

Others make up unbiblical theology to explain why someone is not being healed. They explain that God is using sickness to perfect them. At the core of this argument is a misunderstanding of the source of sickness. Acts chapter 10 and verse 38 gives a clear picture of what spiritual force is doing what:

> *how God anointed Jesus of Nazareth with the Holy Spirit and with power, who went about doing good and healing all who were oppressed by the devil, for God was with Him.*

In this Scripture, we see that Jesus is the One who does good and heals. The devil is the one who oppresses with sickness. God does not use sickness to perfect His people. Sickness and disease are of the devil. Jesus is the Healer. He uses healing to manifest His goodness to a people afflicted with sickness through the cruelties of the devil. Healing is a main attribute of God toward man.

When Jesus walked the earth, He did many signs and wonders. A large part of those recorded were healing miracles. These were used to demonstrate the kindness and goodness of the Lord.

In John chapter 14 and verse 9, Jesus said that He came to manifest the heart of God toward us.

> *Jesus said to him, "Have I been with you so long, and*
> *yet you have not known Me, Philip? He who has seen*
> *Me has seen the Father; so how can you say, 'Show us*
> *the Father'?"*

Jesus' words to Philip were filled with amazement. He was astonished that Philip did not yet recognize that Jesus was a living demonstration of God to the human race. Jesus was showing mankind a different view of God than they had known before: God is our Father, who loves us dearly. His posture toward us is one of kindness, goodness, and love. He uses healing as one of the chief ways to manifest this to us.

If this is God's heart and passion toward us, then why do we see people who aren't healed even though they are seeking healing diligently? They do everything they have been told to do. They attempt to operate in faith. They have the "right" people pray for them. They pursue wholeness and wellness, it would appear, with all their heart. Yet they remain sick and diseased—or even worse, they die prematurely. Is this all just a cruel game, or even a lie? Is this healing business really real? Or are we missing a very important part that could unlock healing for those who haven't yet found it?

As my wife, Mary, and I moved full force into healing several years ago, she had a dream. We had been functioning in healing, holding healing services and equipping others to operate in this realm as well. We were honestly seeing good results and were greatly encouraged. There were those who weren't healed as we prayed for them, but a lot of people were being healed. In the midst of this, Mary had her dream. In the dream, she was told, "If you do not pray for them correctly, they will die." She told me about the dream, and my response to her at that time was, "What does that mean?" I was doing the best I could, praying the way I understood, and yet here the Lord was telling me there's something I'm doing wrong, or at least imperfectly. The dream brought me great frustration. The truth was, some did die. Despite our best efforts, people died prematurely. Disease was able to take them out before their time. I still didn't know what it meant to "pray for them correctly."

Several years after this, God began to bring to me the revelation of "the Courts of Heaven." As I began to understand this third dimension of prayer about which Jesus taught, I saw what it meant to "pray for them correctly." I began to see that the reason people were not healed and died prematurely was because the devil had a legal right to hold them in sickness. If they were to be healed, this legal right had to be revoked in the Courts of Heaven. To fully grasp this, we must understand Jesus' teaching on prayer in the Book of Luke. When Jesus was asked to teach His disciples to pray, He placed prayer in three dimensions or realms. He taught them that prayer was approaching God as Father, Friend, and Judge. We approach God as Father for our own needs (see Luke 11:2). We approach God as Friend for the needs of others (see Luke 11:5-8). We approach God as Judge when we are dealing with an adversary (see Luke 18:1-8). The purpose of the adversary is to deny you what is rightfully yours! Healing is ours by covenant with God. The word *adversary* is the Greek word *antidikos*, and it means "one who brings a lawsuit." In other words, it is a legal position from which a case is presented in a court setting. The woman's request in the story Jesus told was for the judge to dismiss the case that was against her. The unjust judge in the parable agreed to do so because of the woman's persistent presentation of her case. The moral of the story is "if this woman can get a verdict in her favor from the unjust judge, how much more will God render a righteous verdict in our favor as the ultimate Judge!"

Many times, the reason people are not healed is because there is a case against them in the legal realm of the spirit. The devil has found some issue he is using to allow sickness to stay attached to them. If we are to see healing manifest, we must deal with the legal case against them in the spirit realm. To do this, we must not just approach the Father and/or Friend. We must approach God as Judge and see verdicts rendered that undo any and every case against us. This is the purpose of this book. We will learn and be empowered to go into the Courts of Heaven and see healing revealed.

My word of encouragement to any who are sick and not yet healed is, there is hope. Through this book, I believe the Holy Spirit will uncover anything resisting all that Jesus died for you to have. Every legal issue in your life, your bloodline, and any other arena will be answered and removed. The healing Jesus died for you to have can and will manifest. The Judge awaits your action to render verdicts that will set into place healing for you!

CHAPTER 1

THE COURTS OF HEAVEN AND HEALING

A MINISTER FRIEND OF MINE NAME RAY AUSTIN, WHO IS a Methodist pastor, was beset by tumors and bleeding in his pituitary gland. It came out of the blue with intense pain and trauma. The pain in his head was so intense that he could only sleep for ten minutes at a time. The pain would then wake him up. This went on for an extended period of time. The doctors told him at first that this was the pain of a stage 4 cancer victim even though the tumor was benign. They later adjusted their statement and told him this was the worst pain known to man. There was much prayer that was activated for him, yet the situation only worsened and there was no healing. Nothing the doctors did brought any relief. They had no ability even to manage the pain.

In the midst of this situation, I felt led to call Ray and pray with him over the phone. As I did, I experienced a tremendous burden of intercession. I began to lead Ray into the Courts of Heaven. We dealt with any sin, transgression, and iniquity that the devil could be using to bring this suffering on him. By the way, if none of these are present and giving the devil legal rights, then we can just appeal to God as Father or even Friend. God's merciful and gracious heart will move on our behalf. But if there is legal ground from which the devil is working, we must get it revoked and removed. In Ray's case, we especially zeroed in on anything in his ancestry where a covenant was made with any demonic power. Ray is of African descent. As a result of this, we dealt with any covenant or agreement made with demonic gods by those in his history. We asked for the blood of the Lamb to annul these covenants. We requested that any place Ray's name or his family's name was on an altar, that it be removed. As a good friend from Nigeria told me, "Every African understands altars." In African history, cities are dedicated to demonic entities. There is at least an altar in the spirit realm, if not the natural, that exists. On these altars are the names of the people in these cities that were dedicated to demonic gods. The result is that the gods claim these people and their bloodlines for themselves. They assert that this gives them the right to bring curses, sickness, tragedies, and troubles to them. This is why bad things can happen to good people. In the realm of healing, this is why people many times don't get permanently healed and well when prayed for. We sought to remove and have revoked any and every legal right of the devil to torment Ray with this sickness and disease. Ray experienced a measure of relief as we dealt with these legal issues before God's court.

Later that night, the pain woke Ray up again. It probably had been around twelve hours since we prayed. As Ray got up in intense pain, he simply began to pray again and ask God to heal him. This time Ray laid down on the couch in his living room. The next thing he knew he heard his neighbors leaving for work. Ray realized that he had been asleep for several hours, which he had not done in several weeks. Then he realized he had no pain. He checked things out for just a little while and then went into the bedroom where Jodie, his wife, was sleeping. He woke her up and announced, "God has healed me!" He then explained what had happened. As the reality of what had been done began to impact them, they started crying, laughing, and rejoicing at the goodness of God, which had manifested itself to them in an amazing way.

Here's the question: Why did Ray's prayer in those early morning hours bring a result that all the other times had not? Did God suddenly decide He loved Ray? Did Ray and everyone else finally pray enough so that God was convinced and healed him? Or did something legal that the devil was using against Ray get revoked and removed so the heart of God toward him could be manifested? This is what I believe, and so does Ray. After we dealt with any possible covenantal right of the devil against Ray, God was free to heal him. Up until this time, the devil, before the Courts of Heaven, was demanding his rights to afflict Ray with this condition. Once the blood of Jesus removed these things, God's passion toward Ray could manifest. It wasn't enough to appeal to the Fatherhood of God or even the Friendship of Jesus. We needed to go before God as Judge and deal with the legal issue stopping the healing. Getting things legally in place in the spirit allowed God to answer Ray's prayer.

As I mentioned earlier, the devil can use sin, transgression, and iniquity as legal rights against our health and us. David spoke of these three words in Psalms chapter 32, verses 1 through 3:

> *Blessed is he whose transgression is forgiven, whose sin is covered. blessed is the man to whom the Lord does not impute iniquity, and in whose spirit there is no deceit. When I kept silent, my bones grew old through my groaning all the day long.*

Notice that David attributed his "bones growing old," a reference to sickness and disease, to his refusal to deal with sin, transgression, and iniquity. But once David repented and experienced forgiveness, his body was restored. God was not afflicting David with sickness because of his sin. The devil was using this as a legal right to bring sickness against him. James chapter 1, verses 13 and 17, tell us the nature and heart of God. Verse 13 says:

> *Let no one say when he is tempted, "I am tempted by God"; for God cannot be tempted by evil, nor does He Himself tempt anyone.*

God does not use evil. It is against His very nature and person to do such a thing. Sickness is not of God. Again, sickness is the tool and oppression of the devil. James continues in verse 17 by declaring:

*Every good gift and every perfect gift is from above,
and comes down from the Father of lights, with whom
there is no variation or shadow of turning.*

God's nature is consistent and without variation. Only good and perfect gifts come from God. God is incapable of bringing evil, and this includes sickness. There is no darkness in Him. There isn't even a shadow.

When David spoke of his "bones growing old" because of his sin, transgression, or iniquity, he was not saying that God was doing this. It was the devil taking advantage of David's present status in the spirit to bring this weakened physical condition. David's repentance took away the legal rights of the devil and allowed healing and restoration to come.

I have dealt with these issues of sin, transgression, and iniquity in my earlier books on the Courts of Heaven. Let's look at these problems now, though, from the healing perspective of healing. These are the three primary things the devil uses to build cases against us that allow sickness to attack us. Remember, the devil operates from a legal perspective. First Peter chapter 5 and verse 8 speaks of this position:

Be sober, be vigilant; because your adversary the devil walks about like a roaring lion, seeking whom he may devour.

Here again the word *adversary* is the Greek word *antidikos*. This word means "an opponent in a lawsuit." It is made up of two words, *anti* and *dikos. Anti* means "instead of" or "in the place of." We also know *anti* means "to be against." The word *dikos* means "rights as self-evident." So, the words together mean "to stand against rights" or "what is rightfully ours." The adversary is one who brings a lawsuit to take away and deny what is rightfully ours. This is very clearly the tactic of the devil. Healing is what belongs to us legally. We will see this in the next chapter. Suffice it to say for now that healing is the children's bread.

Jesus spoke of this in Mark chapter 7, verses 26 through 27. A Gentile woman came to Jesus desiring healing and deliverance for her daughter. Jesus denied her at first because she wasn't a Jew. The New Covenant had not yet been put into place by Jesus' work on the cross. The Old Covenant, which was for the Jewish people alone, was still in operation. As a result of this, Jesus makes a profound statement about healing and deliverance:

> *The woman was a Greek, a Syro-Phoenician by birth, and she kept asking Him to cast the demon out of her daughter. But Jesus said to her, "Let the children be filled first, for it is not good to take the children's bread and throw it to the little dogs."*

Jesus calls healing *"the children's bread"* (Mark 7:27). In other words, it is the covenant right of those who belong to God to be healed. If this was true under the Old Covenant, how much more under the New Covenant that is full of better promises (see Heb. 8:6)?

Even though healing is ours as New Testament believers, we still see those who are not being healed. The reason for this is that the devil has built a case against us as the adversary or *antidikos* who is denying us what is rightfully ours. We must know how to deal with him from the legal dimension of the spirit. This means we must approach God as Judge in His judicial system of Heaven and undo every case against us. Before we can do this, however, we must know what he uses to build those cases and deny our healing!

There is one more portion of Scripture we need to investigate to understand the devil's legal maneuvering in the spirit realm. Revelation chapter 12, verses 10 and 11, shows this to us:

> *Then I heard a loud voice saying in heaven, "Now salvation, and strength, and the kingdom of our God, and the power of His Christ have come, for the accuser of our brethren, who accused them before our God day and night, has been cast down. And they overcame him by the blood of the Lamb and by the word of their testimony, and they did not love their lives to the death.*

John the Apostle calls the devil *"the accuser of* [the] *brethren"* (Rev. 12:10). The Greek word for *accuser* is *kategoros*. It means "a complainant at law." So when the Bible speaks of "the accuser of the brethren," it is not speaking of someone slandering you in the natural. It is speaking of the devil's activities in the Courts of Heaven. People can definitely manifest what is going on in the spirit, but this idea is something happening in the unseen realm. The accuser is building cases and presenting them before Heaven's court. This is to secure the right to devour and consume, if possible. It is to deny us what Jesus paid for that is rightfully ours.

Notice that this accuser is destined to be cast down. We are told that this will come by the blood of the Lamb, the word of our testimony, and not loving our lives unto death (see Rev. 12:11). If we are to see the accuser's case against us dismissed, we must employ these three dimensions. We will see how to do this in a later chapter so that we can secure the healing that already belongs to us.

Let's look at the three main things the devil uses to build cases against us to stop our healings. They are sin, transgression, and iniquity. We have seen how these three things contributed to David's body being weakened and afflicted.

Sin is the Hebrew word *chataah*, and it means "an offense." It comes from the word *chet*, which means "a crime and its penalty." It carries a legal connotation. Sin is a legal issue. It grants the devil legal ground to work against us. Again, this is why we are admonished by Peter to guard against granting the devil legal rights to use against us. First Peter chapter 5 and verse 8 tells us this can allow us to be devoured:

> *Be sober, be vigilant; because your adversary the devil walks about like a roaring lion, seeking whom he may devour.*

From his legal place in the spirit, the devil is building cases against us to devour us. This word *devour* is the Greek word *katapino*, and it means "to gulp down entirely." It also means "to drown." He cannot devour at will. He has to discover a legal right to do so. One of the main things the devil uses to devour, gulp down, and consume is sickness. Sin or anything that is an offense to God grants our legal opponent this right. Peter said we must be sober and vigilant not to give him this right!

There are those who would tell us that the devil has lost *all* his legal rights because of the New Covenant established by Jesus.

They would even go so far as to say that I do not realize what grace has done. They would accuse me of putting people back under bondage and even the law by talking about sin, transgression, and iniquity. Yet I would point out that none other than Peter seemed to understand what was happening in the spirit realm. Please realize that Peter is a New Testament apostle. He clearly understood that satan is still operating legally against us. This is why he is telling us to be sober and vigilant. We must not give the devil legal rights or he will use them against us in the Courts of Heaven. If we have given him rights, we must have them revoked so that everything Jesus died for us to have can be ours.

Sin can be connected to the motive or intention of the heart. Jesus understood this when He spoke in Matthew chapter 5, verses 21 and 22, about murder and anger:

> *You have heard that it was said to those of old, "You shall not murder, and whoever murders will be in danger of the judgment." But I say to you that whoever is angry with his brother without a cause shall be in danger of the judgment. And whoever says to his brother, "Raca!" shall be in danger of the council. But whoever says, "You fool!" shall be in danger of hell fire.*

Jesus said that the state of the heart can be more important than the activity. We must guard our heart. Notice that Jesus said that the words spoken from a bitter, angry, and hateful heart can cause legal troubles in the spirit. Anger without a cause can put us in danger of judgment. This is the Greek word *krisis*, and it means "a decision from a tribunal for or against something." Perhaps we have thought of judgment just being in the hereafter. What if this occurs in the spirit realm now? What if our words of anger cause judgments to be rendered against us that grant the devil the right to devour? We must repent so that these rights are revoked. Could it be that we are not being healed because we will not deal with our hearts and our bitterness? There could be a judgment against us in the spirit realm that will not allow everything Jesus died for to manifest in our life. Please, Lord, help us!

As Jesus continued speaking, He said if we say, "Raca" or "you are worthless," we could be in danger of the "council." This word in the Greek is *sunedrion*, and it was used to refer to the Jewish Sanhedrin. It meant "a joint council or a subordinate tribunal." It was a place where legal decisions were made. Again, could it be that Jesus was not just cautioning about the eternal judgment but also about what is currently happening in the legal dimension of the spirit? Could it be that Jesus was saying there is a "council" in Heaven where verdicts are being rendered based on the state of our heart and the words that flow from it? Have our words of ridicule and judgment against others allowed legal things against us to hold us in sickness? We must repent. The last thing Jesus addressed were those who label someone as a "fool." Jesus says these people can be in danger of the eternal punishment of hell. It would appear that the first two were about what can happen to us because of legal rights of the devil to prosecute us. Then Jesus says that hell can be the final legal rendering against us. The motive of our hearts and the words that flow from it are very important.

We see this in the life of Job. As I shared in my other books on the Courts of Heaven, Job went into terrible situations because the devil brought an accusation against him. The accusation is found in Job chapter 1, verses 8 through 12:

> *Then the Lord said to satan, "Have you considered My servant Job, that there is none like him on the earth, a blameless and upright man, one who fears God and shuns evil?" So satan answered the Lord and said, "Does Job fear God for nothing? Have You not made a hedge around him, around his household, and around all that he has on every side? You have blessed the work of his hands, and his possessions have increased in the land. But now, stretch out Your hand and touch all that he has, and he will surely curse You to Your face!" And the Lord said to satan, "Behold, all that he has is in your power; only do not lay a hand on his person." So satan went out from the presence of the Lord.*

The accusation of satan against Job was about the motive and intention of his heart. He accused Job of serving God because of what he could get out of it. The result was the devastating things through which Job had to walk. The case satan brought against Job allowed him to do massive harm to Job. Part of this was sickness and disease. Job chapter 2, verses 6 through 8, tells us that severe boils appeared on Job's body:

> *And the Lord said to satan, "Behold, he is in your hand, but spare his life." So satan went out from the presence of the Lord, and struck Job with painful boils from the sole of his foot to the crown of his head. And*

he took for himself a potsherd with which to scrape himself while he sat in the midst of the ashes.

Based on the case satan brought against Job, the Lord rendered a judgment. Satan could afflict him with disease and sickness but could not take his life. Job's sickness was a result of a legal case satan had against him. The rest of the Book of Job is about this case being answered. Not only does Job get healed, but restoration comes to him twofold (see Job 42:10).

It is quite interesting that in James chapter 5, verses 9 through 11, James speaks from a New Testament perspective about what happened to Job. He connects Job to God as Judge and the Courts of Heaven:

Do not grumble against one another, brethren, lest you be condemned. Behold, the Judge is standing at the door! My brethren, take the prophets, who spoke in the name of the Lord, as an example of suffering and patience. Indeed we count them blessed who endure. You have heard of the perseverance of Job and seen the end intended by the Lord—that the Lord is very compassionate and merciful.

James cautions against grumbling and speaking evil of others. His reasoning is that the Judge is at the door. I take this to mean that God is listening and discerning and judging. Job's ultimate verdict in the Courts of Heaven was that he received compassion and mercy from the Lord. Healing was secured as well as restoration of wealth and prosperity. We must learn to deal with any motive, wound, hurt, or intention that can be used against us in the Courts of Heaven. Our healing could hang in the balance.

The second thing satan uses to build a case against us is transgression. Transgression is the Hebrew word *pasha*. It means "a revolt or rebellion." Transgression comes from a word meaning "to break away from authority." We transgress when we throw off restraints and say, "We don't care what God thinks; we will do this anyway." It's not just about the activity but the attitude attached to it. When the devil finds these kinds of things in our lives, he is able to put together a case against us in the Courts of Heaven.

In regard to sickness, we can see this in the story of the man at the Pool of Bethesda in John chapter 5. In this story, we find a man who is waiting for the stirring of the waters in the pool. It is said that when the waters stir, whoever gets into them first will be made whole. The Scripture says there was a *"great multitude of sick people"* around this pool (John 5:3). This speaks of the desperation of people to be made well. Yet only the first one in the water on a yearly basis was healed. They attributed the stirring of the water to "an angel" (see John 5:4). This seems like a very cruel scenario. Only one in the midst of a multitude would get healed. Some claim that this "angel" that was said to stir the waters could have been a water god. In other words, it was a demonic entity designed to get attention and worship (because this is what they desire—see Matthew 4:8) and to distract from who God really is.

In the midst of this, Jesus comes to a man who has been sick for thirty-eight years and asks him if he wants to be healed. The obvious answer would be yes, wouldn't it? Why would Jesus ask this? If you have had a medical condition for thirty-eight years, there is a strong possibility that your identity is now wrapped up in your sickness. In other words, you wouldn't know who you were without it. It might seem crazy, but people can begin to have emotional connections to their illness. It's what they talk about, think about, and even live for. These people cannot be healed. In fact, this attitude can give the devil the legal right to hold them in their sickness.

Once Jesus affirms that this man desires healing, He speaks the word and the man responds and is healed. Later Jesus finds the man in John chapter 5 and verse 14 and reveals why he was sick in the first place:

> *Afterward Jesus found him in the temple, and said to him, "See, you have been made well. Sin no more, lest a worse thing come upon you."*

Jesus clearly says the man's disease was a result of sin in his life. He admonishes the man to *"sin no more"* or something even worse would come on him (John 5:14). The man's initial condition was a result of the devil having the legal right to afflict him. If he went back to his sin, it would give the devil the legal right to bring something even worse. Matthew chapter 12, verses 43 through 45, shows us the nature of the demonic:

> *When an unclean spirit goes out of a man, he goes through dry places, seeking rest, and finds none. Then he says, "I will return to my house from which I came." And when he comes, he finds it empty, swept, and put in order. Then he goes and takes with him seven other spirits more wicked than himself, and they*

enter and dwell there; and the last state of that man is worse than the first. So shall it also be with this wicked generation.

When the devil's power is broken, he will come back and see if a legal right is being granted to re-enter. If it is, he and seven more wicked spirits will come back to torment and afflict. This is what Jesus is warning this man about. It is possible to get healed but then "lose" your healing because legal rights are granted the devil. We want to maintain everything the Lord has graciously given us.

I don't know what is worse than thirty-eight years of suffering, but something is. Remember, this man couldn't even get himself into the water. So whatever his condition was, it incapacitated him on some level. Jesus lets us know that this particular malady was joined to sin and transgression, giving the devil the legal right to accuse him.

We must repent of anything that is in rebellion against God. When I choose to do what I want to do regardless of what God desires, I am giving satan evidence to build legal cases against me. The purpose of the devil's temptation is to gain evidence against us in the Courts of Heaven. In Matthew chapter 4 and verse 3, we see satan tempting Jesus:

Now when the tempter came to Him, he said, "If You are the Son of God, command that these stones become bread."

The purpose of his temptation was to be able to accuse Jesus in the Courts of Heaven and deny Him the right to be our Savior. This is the way the devil works. He tempts us, gets us to fall, and then uses it against us in God's court. This is why Peter encouraged us to be on guard. Remember again First Peter chapter 5 and verse 8:

> Be sober, be vigilant; because your adversary the devil walks about like a roaring lion, seeking whom he may devour.

We are to protect ourselves from our adversary the devil—our legal opponent who continually seeks out legal rights to devour. We must not sin, but if we do, we must repent quickly of every rebellion that allowed it. Otherwise the devil can use this to bring sickness and disease against us.

The other thing in the spirit realm used to build legal cases against us to afflict us with disease is *iniquity*. It is the Hebrew word *avon*. It means "perversity." It comes from a word meaning "to be crooked." This word is associated with the sins in our heritage. Jeremiah chapter 14 and verse 20 shows a repentance of personal sins and the iniquities of the fathers:

> We acknowledge, O Lord, our wickedness and the iniquity of our fathers, for we have sinned against You.

It is the iniquity of the fathers that causes a perversion of our desires and longings. Iniquities can twist our very nature. We feel pulls of temptation based on what our fathers have allowed. It gives the devil the legal right to work against us.

This must have been a common thought in the times of Jesus. The disciples bring it up as a reason why a man was born in a certain condition. John chapter 9, verses 1 through 7, chronicles the healing of a blind man:

> *Now as Jesus passed by, He saw a man who was blind from birth. And His disciples asked Him, saying, "Rabbi, who sinned, this man or his parents, that he was born blind?"*
>
> *Jesus answered, "Neither this man nor his parents sinned, but that the works of God should be revealed in him. I must work the works of Him who sent Me while it is day; the night is coming when no one can work. As long as I am in the world, I am the light of the world."*
>
> *When He had said these things, He spat on the ground and made clay with the saliva; and He anointed the eyes of the blind man with the clay. And He said to him, "Go, wash in the pool of Siloam" (which is translated, Sent). So he went and washed, and came back seeing.*

The disciples felt it was some kind of sin in this man's history that allowed him to be born unable to see. Jesus said that wasn't the case in this situation. Many people interpret this passage to mean that the sins of previous generations cannot cause sickness in a person. I've never thought this was what Jesus was saying. I believe Jesus was referring to this individual circumstance. He was saying, "In this case, it wasn't generational issues that caused the blindness." Yet the possibility does exist that the iniquity in a person's ancestry can give the devil the legal right to bring such things into being. We must be discerning when dealing with sickness and disease. This is especially true when people are seeking sincerely yet are not being healed. Searching out the legal issue that the devil is using to hold someone in a place of affliction can be essential to that person being healed. This is what I now understand the Lord meant when He said to my wife, "You must pray for them correctly or they will die."

In the chapters to come, we will examine some issues in our bloodline that satan can use to hold us legally in a place of sickness. If we can discern his case against us, we can then revoke it by the blood of Jesus in the Courts of Heaven. Once this occurs, the devil no longer has a legal right to keep us in this place. We are free to receive fully everything Jesus died for us to have.

In the next chapter, we will see the legal work of Jesus on the cross and the verdict that resulted. This is absolutely necessary to recognizing what we are now doing in the Courts of Heaven. Get ready—healing is close, even at hand! Here is a prayer to begin to be positioned in His courts:

> *Lord, thank You for the third dimension of prayer, whereby we can come before You as Judge. Lord, I ask for Your help to stand before You in the court system of Heaven and present my case. I thank You that You help me take everything You have done and present it before Your courts. As I do, let every accusation against me be removed, and allow healing to flow into our lives. In Jesus' name. Amen.*

CHAPTER 2

THE VERDICT OF JESUS' CROSS

SEVERAL YEARS AGO, A YOUNG LADY AND HER HUSBAND came to me. She had been diagnosed with lupus. At the time they came, we were doing an extended fast. As a church, we were praying three times a day. We were meeting in prayer in the early morning, at noon, and then also in the evening. This lady called the offices and asked if she could make an appointment for me to pray for healing for the lupus with which she had been diagnosed. I suggested that she and her husband come to the noon prayer meeting.

They showed up right as the prayer meeting was ending. It ended up just being the two of them with my son Adam and me in the sanctuary, where we had been praying. I was very tired from the fast we were on and having just led the prayer meeting. I didn't feel inspired or anointed. As the lady approached me, I laid my hand on her head and began to pray as best I could in my weakened state. I had prayed for just a short time when I heard this faint whisper in my spirit: "Rebuke the devil." So I quietly said, "Satan, I rebuke you and command you to go." The very moment I said this, the lady's feet went straight up in the air. She landed on her back and shoulders with great force. Her eyes rolled back into her sockets, showing only murky white. A guttural voice came from the very petite woman. Speaking to me, it said, "I judge you." I was instantly transformed from a weak, tired pastor to an energized warrior of God. I quickly repositioned myself on the floor beside the woman. Her husband was backing away in shock at what was happening to his wife. My son was standing, watching in dismay. As I hit the floor beside her, I said to the demon force clearly coming from her, "You judge me? I judge you by the blood of Jesus." The thing in her suddenly went silent. I began the process of getting the demon out and her free. We did in fact do this, and she reported her condition as healed and restored.

I have never forgotten that encounter. I didn't understand the Courts of Heaven then. As I developed an awareness of them, this incident came back to me. I realized this demon power was trying to use something legal to keep me from casting it out and getting this woman healed. Its problem was that I had a revelation of Jesus, His blood, and what He did on the cross! The cross of Jesus is at its core a legal transaction. In fact, it is the greatest legal transaction in history. When we function in the Courts of Heaven, we are operating from the finished work of Jesus on His cross. Jesus' atoning work on the cross is the answer to any and every case the devil would try to use against us. If we are going to be successful in unlocking healing from the Courts of Heaven, we must understand the cross.

Isaiah chapter 53, verses 1 through 6, provides a glimpse of what Jesus accomplished on the cross:

> *Who has believed our report? And to whom has the arm of the Lord been revealed? For He shall grow up before Him as a tender plant, and as a root out of dry ground. He has no form or comeliness; and when we see Him, there is no beauty that we should desire Him. He is despised and rejected by men, a Man of sorrows and acquainted with grief. And we hid, as it were, our faces from Him; He was despised, and we did not esteem Him. Surely He has borne our griefs and carried our sorrows; yet we esteemed Him stricken, smitten by God, and afflicted. But He was wounded for our transgressions, He was bruised for our iniquities; the chastisement for our peace was upon Him, and by His stripes we are healed. All we like sheep have gone astray; we have turned, every one, to his own way; and the Lord has laid on Him the iniquity of us all.*

Prophetically looking through the centuries, Isaiah sees what Jesus would accomplish on the cross and declares a transaction and trade that would change the course of history. He observes the torment of the cross and speaks of Jesus being rejected by men. He sees mankind not understanding the price Jesus was paying on the cross for our sins. He says that we even thought God was smiting Him under His judgment. Yet Jesus' work on the cross would allow the greatest legal transaction of history. It would grant God the legal right He needed to forgive and cleanse our sin forever. It would also release healing to us in every dimension of our lives. Furthermore, it would be the basis for all restoration. Not only would we as people be able to be legally reclaimed, but even creation would be restored. We can never underestimate the power of the cross!

There are at least four things that Isaiah prophetically saw that the cross would accomplish. The first thing mentioned is that Jesus and His cross would bear our grief and carry our sorrows. When we read this, we think Jesus came to deliver us from some sadness, but that is not what this Scripture is saying. The word *grief* in Hebrew is *choliy*, and it means "disease, malady, calamity, and sickness." The word *sorrow* is the Hebrew word *makob*, and it means "to have pain, to make sore, to feel pain." So, Jesus died on the cross to carry away our sicknesses, diseases, maladies, and pain. One of His main purposes for dying on the cross was to declare sickness illegal. As far as God is concerned, because of what Jesus did, disease, pain, and sickness are illegal and have no right to operate!

When this Scripture is quoted in the New Testament, the translators make it clearer. Matthew chapter 8, verses 16 and 17, emphasizes this word from Isaiah with more clarity:

> *When evening had come, they brought to Him many*
> *who were demon-possessed. And He cast out the spir-*
> *its with a word, and healed all who were sick, that*

*it might be fulfilled which was spoken by Isaiah the
prophet, saying: "He Himself took our infirmities and
bore our sicknesses."*

Jesus healed *"all who were sick"* to show He was the One Isaiah
was speaking of. Even though this was before the physical cross,
Jesus had already died before the foundations of the earth. In the
spirit realm, it was legal for Him to release healing to them all
because the cross had made it illegal for sickness to operate! If this
was true before the literal cross, how much more afterward?

Peter perceived this truth and proclaimed it in his writings.
First Peter chapter 2 and verse 24 declares that we are *now* healed:

*who Himself bore our sins in His own body on the
tree, that we, having died to sins, might live for righteousness—by whose stripes you were healed.*

Peter was aware that when Jesus died on the cross, everything
legal that was necessary for healing was now accomplished. This is
why Jesus declared while on the cross, *"It is finished!"* (John 19:30).
This was a legal statement. There was nothing left that satan could
use to prevent the healing of God from coming to those who
belong to Him. Legal things were now in place for a full manifestation of healing and wholeness.

It is important to remember here that the cross was a verdict
rendered. The cross granted God the legal right to proclaim sickness illegal. The additional truth we must factor in is that a verdict
not executed has no power. Even though it has been legally rendered, unless it is acted upon it has no real authority. We will see
in a later chapter how to take the legal decision of the cross and

see it become reality. When this is done, healing is functionally manifested. Let me illustrate using an example from the natural. When someone dies, their will, in effect, is a verdict that must be set into place. There must be an execution of that will before people can get their inheritance. There is an executor that must do their job or else what is in the will won't get into the hands of those for whom it was intended. We must learn how to operate in this dimension to receive what Jesus legally supplied for us on the cross. When we do, the legal provision of the cross will have functional reality.

Many times, the devil will not let go until we force him to in the Courts of Heaven. He will try to maintain his case against us to torment and even kill us with sickness. We will see later some of the things he uses to deny us what is legally ours. When we understand what Jesus did on the cross, we can take the activity of the cross and overcome every accusation against us. This is why Revelation chapter 12, verses 10 and 11, says we overcome the accuser with the blood of the Lamb:

> *Then I heard a loud voice saying in heaven, "Now salvation, and strength, and the kingdom of our God, and the power of His Christ have come, for the accuser of our brethren, who accused them before our God day and night, has been cast down. And they overcame him by the blood of the Lamb and by the word of their testimony, and they did not love their lives to the death...."*

We take the work of Jesus on the cross and use the testimony of the blood to secure the healing Jesus legally provided us. We silence the case of the accuser, or *kategoros*, against us. Remember that the *kategoros* is one who brings a complaint in a judicial system. When his complaint is silenced by the blood, healing can manifest.

Healing is the first thing Isaiah mentions that the cross of Jesus legally secured. Isaiah continues by declaring that Jesus *"was wounded for our transgressions,* [and] *bruised for our iniquities..."* (Isa. 53:5). The cross of Jesus legally dealt with every aspect of our sin. What Jesus did on the cross gave God the legal right to forgive! The Lord always wanted to forgive, but He needed the legal right. This is why in the Old Testament God could only cover the sins or roll them back for a year. The blood of the sacrifice allowed for only a partial and temporary redemption. When Jesus died on the cross and shed His blood, it enabled the Lord not only to legally cover, but to cleanse. Now our sins are forgiven and washed away. We are redeemed, justified, and made righteous by His blood. The heart of the Lord toward us has always been love, mercy, redemption, and forgiveness. He now has a legal right for us to receive fully from His gracious hand. When we obey First John chapter 1 and verse 9, we execute the verdict of the cross for our forgiveness.

If we confess our sins, He is faithful and just to forgive us our sins and to cleanse us from all unrighteousness.

Our confession of sin releases His faithfulness, which speaks of His covenant-keeping nature, and His justice, which speaks of His legal nature, into place. Through our confession we have secured the verdict rendered into place. We are forgiven and cleansed because the verdict of the cross is now executed.

The next thing Isaiah says the cross will do is bring us peace in our emotions and minds. He declares, *"...The chastisement for our peace was upon Him..."* (Isa. 53:5). In other words, Jesus was chastised and tormented so that we could have peace. This is the answer for emotional and mental struggles. The cross of Jesus is a verdict that can bring healing in every area. He took our emotional pain and mental distress and gave us His peace. John chapter 14 and verse 27 shows Jesus telling His disciples that He is giving them His peace:

> *Peace I leave with you, My peace I give to you; not as the world gives do I give to you. Let not your heart be troubled, neither let it be afraid.*

Jesus can give us His peace because of the verdict rendered on the cross against demonic assault on our minds and emotions.

Years ago in my twenties, I went through a hellish experience. I awoke one morning in the early hours while it was still dark. The very presence of evil was in the room. It seemed as if I was staring the devil in the face. I felt like I was losing my mind. It is difficult for me to explain, but I felt like I was hanging on a precipice and if I let go I would fall into a bottomless pit. There was nothing wrong in the natural, just normal life pressures. There was no explanation for what I was experiencing. I tried to talk to some people about it, but they didn't seem to understand. I felt completely alone. All I could do was cry out to the Lord. When I tried to read the Word, it tormented me. I would only see and feel judgment. This went on for months. I managed to function normally in my daily life while all along I was severely tormented in my mind.

One day my pastor came to me and told me he had a dream. In his dream, several demonic powers had me pinned to the ground and were sitting on my chest. They had hatchets in their hand and were striking at my head, trying to split it open and destroy me. He said that as they would strike, I would move my head to dodge their blow. They were barely missing me. When he told me the dream, it resonated with me. This was exactly what was happening. Yet there was no relief.

I asked my mother if there was any mental illness in our family history. She informed me that one of my uncles on my father's side exhibited and was thought to have these issues. I somehow knew what I was experiencing was being empowered by a legal right in my bloodline even though I had no awareness of the Courts of Heaven at this time. I continued to cry out to God. I thought about going to the doctor. I knew that if I did, they would put me on some antidepressant medication. I was certain they would diagnose me as depressed, or something even worse. I would walk outside in absolute terror, trying to hold it all together, and look up at the stars. I was trying to find any kind of significance that I could. I was tormented. I knew the Word of God promised me peace. I knew Jesus was tormented mentally, physically, and emotionally for me to have peace. I began to confess Psalm chapter 56 and verse 3:

Whenever I am afraid, I will trust in You.

I confessed it constantly. I would say it out loud, under my breath, in a whisper. I declared, *"When I am afraid, I will trust in You"* (see Ps. 56:3). Slowly and surely, the fear began to diminish. The torment began to leave. The constant sense of dread started to lift. As I continued to confess the Word, peace came to me. I was accessing the finished works of the cross. I was getting the benefit of what Jesus died for me to have through my confession of faith. My peaceful mind returned, and everything came to rest.

I have thought about that period in my life many times. I'm sure I could have gotten medical help and been placed on medication to correct a chemical imbalance. However, I knew that in my case it was a demonic assault to take away my destiny. I was able to get the power of the cross activated in my life. I want to be very clear though: if someone needs medical help for depression or anything else, please get it. Thank God that He has given doctors wisdom to treat people. I also know that Jesus suffered unimaginable torment so we can have His peace. He took our distresses and gave us His peace that is beyond understanding.

The last thing Isaiah mentions that Jesus accomplished was *"...by His stripes we are healed"* (Isa. 53:5). It's interesting to me that Isaiah begins with Jesus taking away our sickness and disease in healing and finishes with healing as well. Healing is the bookends to everything in between. God at His very core is a healer. It's His nature. When Jesus suffered on the cross, He legally set in place everything necessary for us to access His healing nature. He did in fact "finish" the work. We must now learn how to take what Jesus did and use it legally until every sickness dries up. His sacrifice is all we need.

There is one more thing about the cross that I would like us to see. Remember Paul showed us in First Corinthians chapter 2, verses 1 through 5, the power of the cross:

> *And I, brethren, when I came to you, did not come with excellence of speech or of wisdom declaring to you the testimony of God. For I determined not to know*

anything among you except Jesus Christ and Him crucified. I was with you in weakness, in fear, and in much trembling. And my speech and my preaching were not with persuasive words of human wisdom, but in demonstration of the Spirit and of power, that your faith should not be in the wisdom of men but in the power of God.

Paul determined not to know anything among them except Jesus and Him crucified. He then begins to speak of the necessity of the power of God. It is the message of the cross that releases the power. When the cross is preached, the power will manifest.

There is an Old Testament emblem that represents the cross. It is Passover. Every time you read about the Passover in the Old Testament, you are reading about the cross of Jesus. The Passover was the time when the Passover lamb was killed and offered for Israel's sin. This was a prophetic look at who Jesus would be and what He would do on the cross. In Exodus chapter 12, we see the Lord instituting this Passover. He tells Moses to have the children of Israel kill a lamb per household. They are to apply the blood of that lamb to the doorpost of their dwellings. The reason for this is that God is about to judge Egypt and set His people free after more than four hundred years of bondage. He is going to break the back of this satanic system that is holding His people captive. Exodus chapter 12, verses 7 through 13, unveils the command of the Lord for this Passover:

And they shall take some of the blood and put it on the two doorposts and on the lintel of the houses where they eat it. Then they shall eat the flesh on that night;

roasted in fire, with unleavened bread and with bitter herbs they shall eat it. Do not eat it raw, nor boiled at all with water, but roasted in fire—its head with its legs and its entrails. You shall let none of it remain until morning, and what remains of it until morning you shall burn with fire. And thus you shall eat it: with a belt on your waist, your sandals on your feet, and your staff in your hand. So you shall eat it in haste. It is the Lord's Passover.

For I will pass through the land of Egypt on that night, and will strike all the firstborn in the land of Egypt, both man and beast; and against all the gods of Egypt I will execute judgment: I am the Lord. Now the blood shall be a sign for you on the houses where you are. And when I see the blood, I will pass over you; and the plague shall not be on you to destroy you when I strike the land of Egypt.

The Israelites had two basic commands attached to this Passover. They were to apply the blood of the lamb to the doorpost. This would be a marking or sign that would allow them to escape judgment. As the Lord would judge Egypt from His courts (remember that judgment is an activity of a court), Israel would not be judged. The blood of the Lamb of God is our defense against judgment. The blood gives us what we need to escape judgment and be found innocent. We overcome every accusation against us by the blood of the Lamb (see Rev. 12:10-11).

The second command was to eat the carcass of the roasted lamb whose blood had been applied to their doorpost. The roasted lamb speaks of the torment and torture Jesus went through for us. Jesus, as the Lamb of God, was put through intense suffering for us. All the beating, chastising, and ultimately death was Jesus fulfilling the prophetic picture of that lamb that was roasted.

By eating the lamb they were declaring that they were partaking of all Jesus would accomplish on the cross. They were to eat it with bitter herbs. Perhaps, among other meanings, this speaks of the bitter places we might walk through as we partake of the Lamb and His provisions. Our Christian experience is not always absent of hardship. There are times when we encounter pain and difficulty. These are the bitter herbs with which they were to eat the lamb.

They also were to eat all of it. This means that we are to partake of everything that Jesus is. Many people like the blessing side of Jesus. How about the side of Jesus where He says we must forsake all to completely follow Him (see Luke 14:33)? In other words, we cannot pick and choose the aspects of Jesus we want and leave others out. We must be willing to fully follow and obey as the Holy Spirit empowers us. I believe this must be our heart and attitude to get the full benefits of Jesus' legal activity on the cross.

Furthermore, they were to eat this lamb with their clothes and shoes on and with their staff in their hand. In other words, they had to act like they were going somewhere. These were Jews who had been in captivity in Egypt for 430 years. Yet right then, God was promising them that they were going to leave Egypt by morning. Something that had not happened in 430 years was about to happen overnight. They had to believe this and act like they thought it was about to happen—and it did. They were being told to put confidence in the power of this Passover. God was about to judge all their enemies, and they were going to be free.

Faith is very important to getting the benefits of Jesus and His cross. This is why there were times Jesus said, "Be it unto you according to your faith" (see Matt. 9:29). Everything we get, we get through the faith realm. Faith is when we decide to take God at His word. It is when we choose to let what God says trump all other voices. We believe by revelation the word of the Lord to us. This is why they were to eat this Passover lamb ready to leave. They were symbolically declaring that as they partook of this sacrifice of the lamb, a miracle of deliverance was coming. So often people do not get what the cross has legally provided because they can't get past the foolishness of faith. They allow their past experiences or logic to overwhelm them. The Apostle Paul even spoke of the foolishness of the cross to some. First Corinthians chapter 1 and verse 18 tells us this:

> *For the message of the cross is foolishness to those who are perishing, but to us who are being saved it is the power of God.*

Notice that those who believe in the cross and Jesus' activities on it are granted power unto salvation. Those who mock or disbelieve perish. It is essential for us to believe what Jesus, as the Lamb of God, did for us on His cross. When we do, we can experience His power that saves us from anything that is against us.

The final thought I want to bring about this Passover is that as they partook of the roasted lamb, healing flowed through the ranks of Israel. Psalm chapter 105, verses 36 and 37, gives us three things the Passover, or the cross in a shadow or prophetic emblem, did for the Jews:

> *He also destroyed all the firstborn in their land, the first of all their strength. He also brought them out with silver and gold, and there was none feeble among His tribes.*

God destroyed their firstborn and gave Israel deliverance from captivity. He also brought them out with prosperity. They had been poor slaves, but overnight they became rich Jews. Prosperity is something that should be believed for. The cross legally destroys the poverty spirit. This passage also says that *"...there was none feeble among* [them]*"* (Ps. 105:37). They were completely healed. There were none who were weak, much less sick or diseased. How could this be with millions of Jews who had served under cruel slavery for centuries? As they ate the roasted lamb on that night, they partook of the life that was to flow from the cross centuries later. In a sense, they ate healing to themselves; that is to say, they appropriated what Jesus would do for them years later.

The blood of the Lamb is for our forgiveness. Through Jesus' blood we are forgiven, redeemed, brought into covenant, protected, and remembered by God. Through His body that was on the cross (the roasted lamb) we are healed. Remember He bore away our sicknesses and carried away our pains in His body as the Lamb. This was all done legally by Jesus' activities on the cross.

When all these Jews, in obedience to God's command, ate the roasted lamb on Passover night, healing flowed through them all. In every household, diseases were instantly healed. Sicknesses and maladies dried up as they put the meat of the lamb into their mouths. As they partook of the provisions of this lamb, wholeness came to an entire nation. What a powerful thing. This was the result of the cross of Jesus in a prophetic symbol. If this can happen from just something that was a sign of what was to come, what can happen from the reality of it? The cross of Jesus is the activity we needed for healing to become ours. It has been purchased, paid for, and legally set in place. We must know how to take advantage of what Jesus has done so we can gain the benefits of it. The cross, sacrifice, and blood of Jesus is all we need to be healed. We must know how to go into the Courts of Heaven and claim what is legally ours. Many of us will have to answer the accusations the devil is trying to use against us to keep us sick. The cross and Jesus' blood is everything we need to get the fullness of what Jesus legally secured. Because of all that Jesus has done as our Passover Lamb, there is no case against us that we cannot win. We can step into the Courts of Heaven and win every time! Here is a prayer to apprehend what Jesus did for us on the cross:

> *Lord as we stand before You, I thank You for all that was accomplished on the cross. Thank You so much for the suffering you endured that legally provided us with healing. We believe that when You died on the cross, You bore away every sickness and carried away all our pains. I also believe that because of the stripes You endured, I am healed. I receive from Your cross the healing flow, and by faith I apprehend it. In Jesus' name. Amen.*

CHAPTER 3

REBELLION AND THE BLOODLINE

REMEMBER THAT THE DEVIL'S POWER TO DEVOUR IS connected to his ability to build legal cases against us (see 1 Peter 5:8). He is the *antidikos*, or "one who brings a lawsuit against us." He uses sin, transgression, and iniquity to secure these rights. The blood of the Lamb in the Courts of Heaven answers all of the devil's accusations. Revelation chapter 12, verses 10 and 11, gives us further insight into this:

> *Then I heard a loud voice saying in heaven, "Now salvation, and strength, and the kingdom of our God, and the power of His Christ have come, for the accuser of our brethren, who accused them before our God*

day and night, has been cast down. And they over-
came him by the blood of the Lamb and by the word
of their testimony, and they did not love their lives to
the death."

Satan is called *"the accuser of* [the] *brethren"* (Rev. 12:10). You will remember that as the accuser, or *katagoros*, he is a complainant at law. He is accusing us day and night. This means he is perpetually presenting cases against us, seeking to gain the legal right to devour us.

To present a case in a court you must have evidence. One of the main sources that satan uses to get evidence against us is our bloodline. Sin, transgression, and the rebellions in which our forefathers have walked provide this for the satanic realm. We must recognize this and ask the Holy Spirit to provide any understanding we need. When dealing with sickness that does not seem to respond to the healing that is rightfully ours, we should examine this area. Hidden within our bloodline could be the legal issue satan is using.

Many people point out that bloodline issues are not something with which New Testament believers should be concerned. We will get into the spiritual transactions concerning this later. Suffice it to say here that the New Testament does place an emphasis on natural bloodlines. For instance, Jesus warned the religious leaders that the sin of their forefathers made them guilty. Matthew chapter 23, verses 29 through 33, shows Jesus speaking strongly to these leaders:

Woe to you, scribes and Pharisees, hypocrites! Because
you build the tombs of the prophets and adorn the

*monuments of the righteous, and say, "If we had lived
in the days of our fathers, we would not have been
partakers with them in the blood of the prophets."
Therefore you are witnesses against yourselves that
you are sons of those who murdered the prophets. Fill
up, then, the measure of your fathers' guilt. Serpents,
brood of vipers! How can you escape the condemnation
of hell?* (Matthew 23:29-33)

Jesus taunted them with the fact that their fathers had killed
the prophets. As a result of their fathers' actions, they were guilty
as well. Jesus realized that unless they dealt with the issues in their
bloodline, they would suffer the consequences of their fathers' sins.
He actually said for them to *"fill up,"* or complete their fathers'
sins (Matt. 23:32). This means that they were to fulfill anything
left out so that legally complete judgment could come. It was their
fathers' sins mixed with their present sin that would allow judgment to fall legally. This happened to them as a nation in A.D. 70
when Jerusalem was destroyed and the temple annihilated. This
occurred not just because they rejected and killed Jesus, but also
because of what their fathers had done to the prophets.

Jesus continues in Matthew chapter 23, verses 34 and 35, by
showing them the results of both their own and their fathers' sin:

*Therefore, indeed, I send you prophets, wise men, and
scribes: some of them you will kill and crucify, and
some of them you will scourge in your synagogues and
persecute from city to city, that on you may come all
the righteous blood shed on the earth, from the blood
of righteous Abel to the blood of Zechariah, son of*

Berechiah, whom you murdered between the temple and the altar.

Notice that Jesus says to the present generation that they are guilty of murdering all the prophets from Abel to Zechariah. The people to whom Jesus is speaking weren't even alive when these prophets died, and yet they are being declared guilty of these horrible sins. This is because their fathers had actually committed the crimes. As far as Jesus was concerned, this made them guilty as well. Jesus understood the nature of the spirit realm. He knew that the sins of the fathers would be used against the children legally. They needed to repent of not just their sin, but also the iniquity of the fathers.

In Romans chapter 11, verses 28 and 29, we see a New Testament bloodline emphasis:

Concerning the gospel they are enemies for your sake, but concerning the election they are beloved for the sake of the fathers. For the gifts and the calling of God are irrevocable.

Paul says the Jews are beloved for the fathers' sake. In other words, God is paying attention to the Jews as a people because of the covenant He made with their fathers. They will have opportunity for salvation because of their bloodline and who their fathers were. Bloodlines can determine the favor, privileges, and blessings afforded us. God honors bloodlines. Satan seeks to use them legally against us.

Another Scripture that reveals this is Romans chapter 3, verses 1 and 2:

What advantage then has the Jew, or what is the profit of circumcision? Much in every way! Chiefly because to them were committed the oracles of God.

Paul says the Jews have an advantage and a profit because of their bloodline. The fact that God trusted them with His word and principles causes God to honor them as a people. This is a bloodline issue. The spirit dimension pays attention to bloodlines. God legally honors and blesses on the bases of bloodlines. The devil seeks the legal right to devour, hinder, and destroy as a result of bloodlines. What our fathers have done does have a legal effect in the spirit realm over us.

I have discovered there are at least five distinct realms connected to our bloodlines. These can provide the devil with testimony or evidence against us. These five are rebellion, trades, covenants, dedications, and words. Some of these will overlap with each other. It is important, though, that we can see each one. They can then be legally removed through the blood of the Lamb. Through faith we can take what Jesus did for us and dissolve the legal issue that satan would use to torment us with sickness. Once the legal issue is revoked and removed, healing can manifest.

I will first mention rebellion in our bloodline that is used legally by satan. This is the outright sin committed by our ancestors when they, in rebellion against God, walked contrary to Him and His ways. We are told in First Samuel chapter 15 and verse 23 that rebellion and stubbornness connect us to demonic things:

For rebellion is as the sin of witchcraft, and stubbornness is as iniquity and idolatry. Because you have rejected the word of the Lord, He also has rejected you from being king.

If people in our bloodlines walked in rebellion against the Lord, this can give the devil the legal right to afflict with sickness. Witchcraft is the agreement with demon powers. Idolatry is the worship of something that is empowered by demons. Any time either of these things is done, there is an agreement with demon powers that legally invites their influence. We must repent of any time our ancestors walked in rebellion and sinned against God.

We see this in the life of Asa, king of Judah. Asa served God and had good success. Yet the success seemed to cause arrogance and pride to come into his life. Later on, a prophet confronts Asa concerning his reliance on the flesh rather than God. Asa had counted on other nations, rather than the Lord, to defend Israel. The prophet came to call Asa to repentance concerning his misappropriated confidence. In Second Chronicles chapter 16 and verse 10, we see Asa's response to him:

> *Then Asa was angry with the seer, and put him in prison, for he was enraged at him because of this. And Asa oppressed some of the people at that time.*

Instead of repenting, Asa punishes this seer who came with the prophetic word of the Lord to correct him. He also attacks some of the people in his kingdom—probably those who disagreed with his decisions.

In the next verses, the Bible reveals that a sickness beset Asa. The writer seemingly is connecting Asa's sin and rebellion to the sickness that befell him. Second Chronicles chapter 16, verses 12 and 13, reveals how Asa develops a malady in his feet that ultimately kills him:

> *And in the thirty-ninth year of his reign, Asa became diseased in his feet, and his malady was severe; yet in his disease he did not seek the Lord, but the physicians. So Asa rested with his fathers; he died in the forty-first year of his reign.*

Notice that Asa's sin of not trusting the Lord potentially allowed the sickness to continue because he did not seek the Lord in his condition. We know that God does not afflict with sickness. We have established this. The Lord is good. However, the devil does take advantage of our sin and rebellion to legally be able to harass us with disease. Our rebellion can give him the legal right to bring sickness against us. Repentance is necessary to revoke that right. Yet in Asa's case, instead of repenting, he continued in his rebellion until he died. We must learn to walk in the fear of the Lord and be tender before the Lord. This will allow us to repent rather than harden our hearts. We must also deal with any rebellion in our bloodline that is allowing the devil the legal right to torment us with maladies. The rebellion in our bloodline can make us susceptible to rebellion ourselves. We can find a propensity in ourselves toward rebellion because of the rebellion of our ancestors.

Please be aware that I am not implying we sin or are in rebellion against God if we go to doctors. This is not what the Scripture is saying or implying. I believe we should always make the Lord the One we trust for healing. It is not wrong, however, to believe that

God can use a doctor to bring healing. The Lord may use natural means or supernatural means to bring healing. All healing comes from the Lord, who is Jehovah Rapha, the Lord Who Heals. Asa's problem was in his rebellion. He did not seek the Lord. He put his confidence in the flesh apart from God. This was rebellion against the Lord in a severe way. It was the continuation of a lifestyle and attitude in which he had walked for many years.

Exodus chapter 15 and verse 26 promises that God, through His nature as healer, will heal His people as they walk obediently before Him:

> ...If you diligently heed the voice of the Lord your God and do what is right in His sight, give ear to His commandments and keep all His statutes, I will put none of the diseases on you which I have brought on the Egyptians. For I am the Lord who heals you.

Notice how in these lines God says that if His people heed His voice, do what is right in His sight, give ear to His commandments, and keep all His statutes, He will see to it that the sickness of Egypt will not touch them. He will reveal Himself as Jehovah Rapha, the Lord Who Heals. So if we, or those in our bloodline, walk in rebellion against the Lord, it gives the devil a legal right to build cases against us and resist our healing. We must know how to repent and ask for the blood of Jesus to speak for us before His courts.

Hebrews chapter 12 and verse 24 tells us that the blood of Jesus is speaking or releasing testimony on our behalf in the Courts of Heaven:

to Jesus the Mediator of the new covenant, and to the
blood of sprinkling that speaks better things than that
of Abel.

Everything mentioned in Hebrews chapter 12, verses 22 through 24, is legal in nature. It speaks of *"God the Judge of all"* (Heb. 12:23). It talks of *"the Mediator of the new covenant"* (Heb. 12:24). It mentions *"the spirits of just men made perfect,"* which is a reference to the *"great...cloud of witnesses"* in Hebrews 12:1 (Heb. 12:23,1). The word *witnesses* here is the Greek word *martus,* and it means "a judicial witness." Those who have already died and are in Heaven have a judicial place in the Courts of Heaven. They are releasing testimony that allows God to move legally from the Courts of Heaven. They are still engaged in activities to ensure that what they lived and gave their lives for becomes reality. It is up to us to agree with Heaven as much as we can. When we do, we see Heaven manifested on the earth.

The blood of Jesus is one of the voices speaking. When we repent for any and all sin and unrighteousness, we activate and agree with the voice of the blood. The blood of Jesus cleanses us from all uncleanness and unrighteousness. First John chapter 1 and verse 7 tells us that as we walk with the Lord, the blood actually "keeps on cleansing" us:

> *But if we walk in the light as He is in the light, we*
> *have fellowship with one another, and the blood of*
> *Jesus Christ His Son cleanses us from all sin.*

In the Greek, this verse literally speaks and implies that the blood has an ongoing cleansing effect in our lives. This makes sense because in Hebrews 12:24, the blood is speaking. It is not just something that spoke, but it continues to speak and bear witness to us. This consistent and persistent speaking allows there to be a cleansing that continues to free us from uncleanness and fashion us into His image! This is the power of the blood of Jesus.

I believe that not only does the voice of the blood cleanse, protect, guard, and grant entrance into His presence, but it also causes God to remember us! The voice of the blood testifies that we are in covenant with the Lord, and therefore God remembers us. Jesus' blood is the blood of the covenant! I pray quite often, "Thank You, Lord, for remembering me because of the blood." I am agreeing with the testimony of the blood. When I do, I cease to be just a human going to Heaven. I am now one saying, "Lord, let me have an impact with my life. Remember me and use me for Your glory. Fulfill Your promises to me."

The Bible says that God remembered Noah. In Genesis chapter 8 and verse 1, we see the Lord calling to mind Noah:

Then God remembered Noah, and every living thing, and all the animals that were with him in the ark. And God made a wind to pass over the earth, and the waters subsided.

God "remembering" is not about Him logically being aware of us. How could God forget Noah? He and his family are the only ones left alive on the earth. So, God remembering was not simply about awareness; it was about the remembering of His purpose and intent in their lives. It was about the specialness of God paying attention to them. It was about God posturing Himself to respond to them! This is what the blood does in our behalf. As the blood speaks of us to the Lord, it causes us to be remembered before Him. This is why I say before the Lord, "I agree with the voice of the blood of Jesus!"

Understanding the power of the blood is essential to dealing with my personal rebellion and the rebellion associated with my bloodline. When I repent and agree with the testimony of Jesus' blood, I am forgiven. Additionally, my bloodline is cleansed. Any case the devil has against me is revoked. The legal right that satan would have been using against me is now removed. I am free to receive the healing Jesus died for me to have.

There are four areas the Lord told the children of Israel that they needed to be careful not to rebel against. Again, we see these in Exodus chapter 15 and verse 26:

> ...If you diligently heed the voice of the Lord your God and do what is right in His sight, give ear to His commandments and keep all His statutes, I will put none of the diseases on you which I have brought on the Egyptians. For I am the Lord who heals you.

First, we must heed the "voice" of the Lord. This means that we must pay attention to the living word spoken to us from the Lord. If we have heard the Lord and disregarded what He said, we have rebelled. There are times when God gives us a specific word that we must obey. Perhaps it was a command for us to do something we didn't want to do. This act of disobedience to God's spoken word can grant the devil the legal right to afflict us.

Also, many times in Scripture people seeking healing were given a word from the voice of the Lord that they had to obey in order to secure their health. We see this in both the Old and New Testament. Naaman, who was a leper, was told to go and dip in the river Jordan seven times. His prejudice against the Jewish people and his assumption of how the healing would come almost caused him to rebel. We see this in Second Kings chapter 5, verses 10 through 14:

> *And Elisha sent a messenger to him, saying, "Go and wash in the Jordan seven times, and your flesh shall be restored to you, and you shall be clean." But Naaman became furious, and went away and said, "Indeed, I said to myself, 'He will surely come out to me, and stand and call on the name of the Lord his God, and wave his hand over the place, and heal the leprosy.' Are not the Abanah and the Pharpar, the rivers of Damascus, better than all the waters of Israel? Could I not wash in them and be clean?" So he turned and went away in a rage. And his servants came near and spoke to him, and said, "My father, if the prophet had told you to do something great, would you not have done it? How much more then, when he says to you, 'Wash, and be clean'?" So he went down and dipped seven times in the Jordan, according to the saying of the man of God; and his flesh was restored like the flesh of a little child, and he was clean.*

When Elisha didn't do it the way Naaman imagined, rebellion rose in his heart. His indignation at the prophet's lack of honor for him, his presumption of how he should be treated, and his bias against Israel almost caused him to rebel and miss the healing. If it hadn't been for the counsel and wisdom of one of his servants, Naaman would have died a leper. The Lord was doing more than just healing Naaman through this command. He was unveiling and dealing with issues of the heart. So often it is issues of the heart that prohibit us from being healed. If we can allow the rebellion in our heart to be surrendered, healing can manifest!

Another story, this one in the New Testament, shows obedience to the "voice" of God as necessary in receiving healing. In John chapter 9, verses 6 and 7, we see Jesus healing a man who was born blind. In this situation, Jesus makes clay from the dirt and His saliva. He applies it to the man's eyes and commands him to go wash in the Pool of Siloam.

> *When He had said these things, He spat on the ground and made clay with the saliva; and He anointed the eyes of the blind man with the clay. And He said to him, "Go, wash in the pool of Siloam."*

Many believe that not only was this man born blind, but he actually had no eyes in the sockets. They believe that Jesus performed a creative miracle by taking the dirt and dust of the earth and completing a prophetic act. The creative power of God manifested and formed eyes in the empty sockets of this man. Remember that God formed Adam from the dust of the earth. Jesus, as the creative power of God, was doing the same thing with the dust of the earth and His saliva. What a glorious God we serve who loves us magnificently!

Jesus then gives the command, *"Go, wash in the Pool of Siloam"* (John 9:7). Even though Jesus had performed a prophetic act, the need for the man to obey the voice of the Lord was necessary. The man, though blind, found his way to the pool and obeyed. The Bible then makes the following statement: he *"came back seeing"* (John 9:7). Wow! The man's obedience to the voice of God caused the miracle to occur. We must do away with every rebellious idea that would deter us from complete obedience. Maybe the Lord will just heal us with no real effort on our part. Maybe He might require something of us as obedience to His voice. We mustn't rebel. We must obey completely and see the glory of God.

The next thing we are cautioned not to rebel against is "[doing] *what is right in His sight"* (Exod. 15:26). This gives us the idea that the Lord is watching and evaluating us. When we recognize this, we begin to walk in the fear of the Lord. Proverbs chapter 5 and verse 21 shows that God is watching the way we live:

> *For the ways of man are before the eyes of the Lord,*
> *and He ponders all his paths.*

We are to endeavor to walk before the Lord, pleasing Him. The word *ponder* is the Hebrew word *palac*, and it means "to roll flat, to revolve, and to weigh." I take this to mean that the Lord is evaluating my walk before Him. He is examining my life by rolling everything out and looking at things from every angle. The Bible tells us in Hebrews chapter 4, verses 12 and 13, that everything is being searched out by Him:

> *For the word of God is living and powerful, and*
> *sharper than any two-edged sword, piercing even*
> *to the division of soul and spirit, and of joints and*
> *marrow, and is a discerner of the thoughts and intents*

of the heart. And there is no creature hidden from His sight, but all things are naked and open to the eyes of Him to whom we must give account.

Through the Word, the Lord searches our soul and spirit, joints and marrow, and discerns intents and thoughts. Everything is naked and open before His eyes. He is looking at everything. The admonition is to walk before His sight and not rebel. We must be aware of His gaze upon our lives and seek to please Him always out of a love relationship.

This kind of awareness gives birth to the fear of the Lord, which was absolutely necessary to creating the atmosphere where miracles could occur. Acts chapter 2 and verse 43 connects the fear of the Lord and signs and wonders occurring:

Then fear came upon every soul, and many wonders and signs were done through the apostles.

When we have an awareness of walking in "His sight," we walk in the fear of the Lord. The atmosphere for signs and wonders is in place. May the Lord help us to walk righteously, reverently, and respectfully before the Lord and His presence. May all rebellion be removed from us and complete surrender be the order.

The next thing mentioned against which we mustn't rebel is the commandments of the Lord. This word *commandments* in the Hebrew is *mitzvah*. It means "a commandment, whether human or divine." It comes from the Hebrew word *tsavah*, which means, among other ideas, "to send a messenger." So, we could say the commandments of the Lord through His messengers are to be obeyed. Often we don't have a problem obeying God's voice when we personally hear it. Yet if God uses someone else to speak to us, we can struggle with hearing it as from the Lord.

We see this even in the days after Jesus' resurrection. In Mark chapter 16 and verse 14, Jesus challenges the unbelief of His disciples when He appears to them in a resurrected form:

> *Later He appeared to the eleven as they sat at the table; and He rebuked their unbelief and hardness of heart, because they did not believe those who had seen Him after He had risen.*

Notice Jesus rebuked the unbelief and hardness of heart because they didn't believe those who had seen Him. How often do we miss visitations from the Lord because we can't receive from those who have "seen" Him? How often does our arrogance, rebellion, and pride prevent someone else who has had a revelation of the Lord from affecting us? We must repent for this. This can legally be used against us by the devil in the Courts of Heaven. This rebellion could stop us from receiving fully what Jesus died for us to have. May we learn to wholly humble ourselves before the Lord and His messengers.

The last thing mentioned is the keeping of statutes (see Exod. 15:26). *Statute* is the Hebrew word *choq*. It means "an appointment" or "a set time." It comes from the idea of enacting laws. Part of the statutes or appointments of the Lord were the Jewish feasts that Israel was commanded to observe every year. They were to appear before the Lord three times a year.

> *Three times you shall keep a feast to Me in the year: You shall keep the Feast of Unleavened Bread.*

They had to appear before the Lord at the Feast of Unleavened Bread. Then Israel came before the Lord at the Feast of Harvest. Then they finished the required feasts with the Feast of Ingathering. In all these gatherings, they had to present themselves before the Lord.

I realize that these feasts have deep prophetic significance. I know they are, at the very least, prophetic emblems. I also realize that many find deep fulfillment in worshiping the Lord with these occasions, even now in our time. I have no problem with this. My heart in this book is to share how the devil uses things in the spirit to disallow the healing God has for us. I believe that we should have "appointed" times of presenting ourselves before the Lord. We should "keep" these times with Him. There is no substitute for being with the Lord and allowing Him the privilege of searching us out. This actually can keep the devil from having legal grounds from which to accuse us. If we are keeping "short accounts" with the Lord, there is nothing for satan to build his case with.

This is why we are exhorted to repent quickly. Revelation chapter 2 and verse 5 commands us to move quickly in repentance:

Remember therefore from where you have fallen; repent and do the first works, or else I will come to you quickly and remove your lampstand from its place— unless you repent.

Jesus said He would come quickly and deal with us if we didn't repent. If He is coming quickly, then this means we should move quickly to repentance. In other words, we shouldn't be lackadaisical about repenting and getting back into line. We must move in the fear of the Lord and seek to be in order before Him. This was one of the purposes of the feast. They were to present themselves before the Lord so that they could be examined before Him. I want to allow the Holy Spirit the right to come and search me out to see if I am lining up with Him. We must give and grant the Lord this right.

To obey in these four areas we must guard against the rebellion that the devil could use to resist our healing. He knows the Lord said that He would be our healer if we did these four things. Again, the first requirement is ready obedience to the voice of the Lord, or His revealed word. The second is doing what is right in the sight of the Lord. We must live our life in view of the Lord. The third is to honor and receive from messengers sent into our lives with the commandments of the Lord. The fourth is to present ourselves for the scrutiny of the Lord so as to allow Him to purge us from anything displeasing. If we will do these four things, we can remove every legal right the devil might have gained through either our rebellion or our ancestors'. We are then free to receive fully the healing Jesus died for us to have. Here's a prayer to help you step into this realm:

> *Lord, I come before You, the Judge of all the earth. I ask for Your courts to open before me. As I enter Your courts, I repent of everything You said would hinder me from being healed. I repent for any and all rebellion in my life. I also repent for any rebellion in my bloodline that would be allowing the devil's case against me. I repent for every place I have not heard and obeyed Your voice. Wherever I have rebelled against Your revealed word, I repent. (If you have an awareness of a specific place, you should repent for that*

here.) I also repent and ask for the blood of Jesus to forgive and cleanse me for every time I have not walked correctly in Your sight. Wherever I might have disregarded Your desires and will, I repent. Please forgive me for this. I also repent for this concerning my bloodline. I repent now for any place I have rebelled against messengers You sent with Your word and commandment. Please, Lord, forgive me and my bloodline. I repent now for being lazy and distracted from presenting myself before You. Every time I disregarded the drawing of Your Holy Spirit to present myself before You, I repent. I ask please, Lord, for Your forgiveness to wash over me. I claim Colossians chapter 2 and verse 14. I declare that the blood of Jesus removes every accusation against me. I declare that anything and everything contrary to me is revoked. Your blood, Lord, removes everything that is against me. I ask that any and all rebellion in me and associated with my bloodline be revoked and removed this instant. I ask that the devil, my adversary, can no longer use it to build cases against me and resist my healing. I ask, Lord, for a full manifestation of my healing to come to me now. Thank You, Lord, for all You did for me through Your death, burial, resurrection, and ascension. I receive it fully now into my life and body through the power of the Holy Spirit.

CHAPTER 4

UNDOING TRADES

YOU MAY NOT HAVE RECOGNIZED THIS, BUT "TRADING" is an activity in the spirit realm. It is possible to trade in God's economy, but also in the devil's realm. Everything is a trade in the spirit world. In fact, the cross of Jesus was the greatest trade of all. Second Corinthians chapter 5 and verse 21 tells us that Jesus traded His righteousness for our sin:

> *For He made Him who knew no sin to be sin for us, that we might become the righteousness of God in Him.*

Jesus became sin for us that we might be the righteousness of God. Wow! Jesus was willing to take His life of righteousness and trade it for us. As a result of this trade, we have salvation.

To understand trading in the spirit world, we need to go back to before creation. Ezekiel chapter 28, verses 14 through 16, speaks of an angelic being that became satan. These verses are commonly thought to be referring to the devil while he was yet in the heavenly courts:

> You were the anointed cherub who covers; I established you; you were on the holy mountain of God; you walked back and forth in the midst of fiery stones. You were perfect in your ways from the day you were created, till iniquity was found in you. By the abundance of your trading you became filled with violence within, and you sinned; therefore I cast you as a profane thing out of the mountain of God; and I destroyed you, O covering cherub, from the midst of the fiery stones.

Satan, while he was yet one of the angelic beings, traded in the spirit realm in which he lived and functioned. This means that there is trading in Heaven. This Scripture is not saying that trading is wrong. It was the iniquity found in him that defiled his trading.

The state of the heart is what determines whether trading is good or bad. Trading is in fact a correct function of the spirit or heavenly realm. The condition of the heart from which the trading is done determines whether it is polluted or not. When satan, as an angelic being, traded with a defiled heart and from iniquity, he *"became filled with violence"* (Ezek. 28:16). This probably speaks of the rebellion he fostered in Heaven. It is thought that a third of the angels followed him (see Rev. 12:3-4). He convinced them to "trade away" their status in Heaven for the promise of something better. The result of this trade was that war and violence broke out in Heaven. Revelation chapter 12, verses 7 through 9, tells us about this war and violence:

And war broke out in heaven: Michael and his angels fought with the dragon; and the dragon and his angels fought, but they did not prevail, nor was a place found for them in heaven any longer. So the great dragon was cast out, that serpent of old, called the devil and satan, who deceives the whole world; he was cast to the earth, and his angels were cast out with him.

Because of this trade made in Heaven, satan and his angels lost the position and place that they previously had. This is *still* the tactic that satan uses against us as the tempter. He seeks to convince us that if we will trade with him, we will increase and gain something. Before we go any deeper into how satan uses trading to hold us in sickness, let me establish trading as a proper activity of the spirit realm.

Just like there are trading floors in the natural realm, there are trading floors in the spirit realm. In the natural, all over the world, people step onto trading floors every day. Wall Street, in New York City, is of course the most famous one. From Wall Street the economies of the world are affected. This is a result of the trading that is going on there. When economies are affected, nations are altered. There is great power in trading from trading floors. There are also trading floors in the spirit as well. Jesus alluded to this in the Parable of the Minas. Luke chapter 19, verses 11 through 25, tells the story of a certain nobleman who commits certain portions of his wealth to his servants. He tells them to "do business" with this currency until he comes back. When he returns, he summons the servants to see how much they have gained with his wealth. The Bible uses a very interesting term in Luke chapter 19 and verse 15. The nobleman wants to see how much they gained through *trading*.

> *And so it was that when he returned, having received the kingdom, he then commanded these servants, to whom he had given the money, to be called to him, that he might know how much every man had gained by trading.*

They were to have taken the currency entrusted to them and *traded* with it to produce something greater.

This is a great principle concerning the accumulation of wealth. However, currency, or something of value, can be much more than natural money. We have been entrusted with time, gifts, energy, favor, anointing, and many other valuable things. How we *trade* with these currencies determines what is produced and gained. We trade every day. Our whole life is a trade. We take the very life that has been granted to us and trade it. This is why Paul, in Second Corinthians chapter 12 and verse 15, speaks of "spending" himself.

> *And I will very gladly spend and be spent for your souls; though the more abundantly I love you, the less I am loved.*

Paul said he would trade himself away for their betterment. In the natural, we take literal currency and trade it for other things. Paul said he was taking spiritual currency and trading for others' benefit.

He saw himself as one who was to take what he had and trade with it for someone else's blessing. He further declared, "Even if you don't see the sacrifice I am making, I'm still willing to make this trade." This was the very spirit of Christ operating in Paul. Just like Jesus traded His life for us, so Paul was willing to trade for the lives of others.

Many times we are stepping onto trading floors in the spirit realm and don't even know it. Our actions, attitudes, sacrifices, and gifts are being acknowledged in the spirit realm. This is what is being implied when the Bible declares in Ezekiel chapter 28 and verse 14 that satan walked on fiery stones before his fall:

> *You were the anointed cherub who covers; I established you; you were on the holy mountain of God; you walked back and forth in the midst of fiery stones.*

The judgment against satan as he was cast out was that he lost his place on the fiery stones or *trading floors of Heaven.* Ezekiel chapter 28 and verse 16 tells us this:

> *By the abundance of your trading you became filled with violence within, and you sinned; therefore I cast you as a profane thing out of the mountain of God; and I destroyed you, O covering cherub, from the midst of the fiery stones.*

God removed satan's rights to function and trade in Heaven. Presently, because the devil knows how Heaven works through trading, he has copied God's system.

In both verses 14 and 16, the "fiery stones" refer to the *trading floors of Heaven.* Satan's "walking back and forth on them" speaks to the fact that he was given rights to function there (see Ezek.

28:14). It's significant that the stones are fiery. When trades are made, if they are accepted they are consumed with fire in Heaven. This is why whatever we do on the earth as we trade must be accepted on the fiery stones of Heaven's courts.

This principle is demonstrated in the life of Noah. When he and his family came out of the ark after the flood, they offered burnt offerings. Genesis chapter 8, verses 20 through 22, shows Noah making a trade:

> *Then Noah built an altar to the Lord, and took of every clean animal and of every clean bird, and offered burnt offerings on the altar. And the Lord smelled a soothing aroma. Then the Lord said in His heart, "I will never again curse the ground for man's sake, although the imagination of man's heart is evil from his youth; nor will I again destroy every living thing as I have done. While the earth remains, seedtime and harvest, cold and heat, winter and summer, and day and night shall not cease."*

Noah had an understanding of the need for his trade to be consumed with fire. He took some of the animals that were on the ark and offered them to God on the fiery stones. He was manifesting on earth what he believed was happening in Heaven as he traded or sacrificed. Trading always involves sacrifice on some level. Real trading in the spirit realm will cost us something. As Noah offered and traded something precious—the few animals left on the earth—the aroma moved God's heart. From the fragrance of this sacrifice upon the fiery stones God rendered a verdict that there would be no more curse! What a powerful example of trading on the fiery stones. We too can step onto the fiery stones of Heaven by faith with our sacrifice. When we do, we are moving onto Heaven's trading floors. Satan has been cast off these floors, but we have been granted access. From this place in the spirit, we can *trade* and see the heart of God moved in powerful ways.

Satan has no power to create, only to copy. When he was cast out of Heaven, he patterned his system after the one in which he once functioned. His system also has trading floors. He tries to get us to step onto these trading floors through temptation. The best example of this is his dealing with Jesus in the wilderness. In Luke chapter 4, verses 5 through 8, we see satan offering Jesus a trade:

> *Then the devil, taking Him up on a high mountain, showed Him all the kingdoms of the world in a moment of time. And the devil said to Him, "All this authority I will give You, and their glory; for this has been delivered to me, and I give it to whomever I wish. Therefore, if You will worship before me, all will be Yours." And Jesus answered and said to him, "Get behind Me, satan! For it is written, 'You shall worship the Lord your God, and Him only you shall serve'."*

Satan offered Jesus dominion of the world if He would worship him. Of course Jesus rejected this trade that satan was offering Him. Satan understood that if he could get Jesus to enter into this trade, satan would have permanent dominion over God's creation. This is one of the main ways satan gains access and even dominion over us. He convinces us to trade with him on his trading floors. If we or our ancestors have made trades with the demonic realm, they can legally claim us. This is where sickness and disease that do not seem to have an answer can come from.

Mary and I have personally experienced this. In my most recent book, *Unlocking Destinies from the Courts of Heaven*, I share a dream about my wife. In my dream, satan's intent was to cause my wife to die prematurely. We took this into the Courts of Heaven and dealt with it there. The result was a sense that we had been able to revoke any legal right of the devil. Even though we felt there had been something strategic done regarding this, I still wondered if everything had been accomplished that was necessary.

A prophet friend of ours had another dream about Mary. In this dream, Mary was sick and diseased and was going to die. This seemed to confirm my suspicions that something still needed to be dealt with. We must understand that the devil's case against us can be multifaceted. We must deal step by step with the issues being used. Going into the Courts of Heaven is not a formula. It is being aware that we desperately need the revelation, empowerment, and help of the Holy Spirit in this process. If we set our heart toward the Lord in genuineness, He will speak to us and reveal to us what we need.

Some people become paranoid concerning this. They start looking for what it is that satan is using against them legally. This is not advisable. We must deal with what we know. If we think there might be something else, we ask God to unveil it. If He doesn't, we need to rest in the fact that at least for the moment, everything being used against us is settled. I lean on Philippians chapter 3 and verse 15:

Therefore let us, as many as are mature, have this mind; and if in anything you think otherwise, God will reveal even this to you.

Paul said if we are immature or have other things we need to deal with, God will reveal them to us. In other words, don't worry about it if God isn't showing it. Trust that if there is something working to our detriment, God, as the loving Father, faithful Friend, and righteous Judge, will show it to us.

The fact that God was again bringing up the intent of the devil to cause Mary to die prematurely told us that there was still something in the case against her. We again set up a time to pray with a prophetic gift. As we prayed, it began to be revealed that someone in Mary's bloodline had made a trade with the spirit of death. The seer/prophetic gift with whom we were working and who had the dream saw a young woman stand up out of a grave. She knew by the Spirit that this young woman had died prematurely. This happened because she had asked to be taken instead of someone else dying. When this young woman did this, she had agreed and made a trade with the spirit of death. She traded her own life to this spirit for the life of someone else who would otherwise have died. The interesting thing about this was that the seer saw this as having occurred in Louisiana or even the New Orleans area. Of course there is much voodoo and witchcraft in that region. What she didn't know is that Mary's ancestors come from those regions and are of French descent. This fit perfectly with what was being seen. This spirit of death that wanted to cause Mary to die prematurely was claiming a right based on the trade this young woman in the vision had made. We had to go into the Courts of Heaven and undo this trade and deny its right to stand against Mary and the women in her bloodline. This is exactly what we did. We immediately felt a shift occur in the atmosphere. The trade had been annulled and disallowed. Therefore, the spirit of death had no legal right to operate. The devil no longer had a right to cause Mary's demise because of a trade with demonic powers made generations ago. Mary is now free to live out the fullness of her destiny written in her books in Heaven.

The legal right of the devil's intent to take Mary out prematurely was based on a trade made in the spirit world. Many times people are sick and dying prematurely because someone made a trade. We must know how to undo these trades. Otherwise all the efforts naturally and spiritually will not bring healing. The devil has a legal right based on the trade to hold and even kill people with sickness. Here are some practical steps to undoing trades on demonic trading floors that have granted the devil legal rights:

- Begin by submitting yourself wholly unto the Lord. You can pray something like this: "Lord, according to Romans chapter 12 and verse 1, I wholly surrender and present myself to You. I yield my body as a living sacrifice unto You, which is my reasonable and acceptable form of worship."

- As you sense that you are surrendered and submitted, you can pray, "Lord, any time I have purposely or by accident made a trade with demonic powers, I repent. I ask that any time this has happened that this trade would be annulled by the blood of Jesus that was shed for me." Should the Lord reveal something specific at this time, repent for it specifically.

- After you have dealt with this on a personal level, you can move on to the bloodline area. You can pray, "Lord, I now repent for any time anyone in my heritage has made a trade with demonic powers. I want nothing to do with this. I ask for any trade made to gain privilege, power, riches, blessings, results, or any other advantage to be undone. I only want that which comes from Jesus Christ."

- Once you have made this statement in the Courts of Heaven you can now declare, "Lord, I give up and I give back anything I have gained from any trade with demonic powers. I don't want any success, prosperity, or blessings that have come from them. I only want what You have given me as my Lord and Savior." You must be willing to give back anything gained through the trade. Otherwise the trade will still stand.

- Now you can pray, "Lord, I ask now that all results against me because of trades with the demonic be reversed. I ask that any sickness and disease operating in my body because of these trades be healed. Lord, I accept what You did for me on the cross. You took away my sickness and bore away my pain. You took my disease and gave me health. I receive now from Your trade made for me on the cross. I accept my healing and receive of the anointing that makes me whole."

We have the right through repentance to ask for the blood of Jesus to annul these trades. When we do, the legal right these trades have granted the devil is revoked. All that Jesus died for us to have we can now access, including the healing life of God. It's time to walk in complete wholeness and health with our God.

CHAPTER 5

ANNULLING COVENANTS

T RADES CREATE COVENANTS. IN ANY AND EVERY covenant made, there is a trade. Even in the marriage covenant, people trade rings and vows and promises. This is what makes the covenants. Once we have dealt with any trades used, we must also undo any covenants that have resulted from the trades. Abraham made covenants with Abimelech that involved trades. Genesis chapter 21 and verse 27 shows Abraham trading with Abimelech and making a covenant:

> *So Abraham took sheep and oxen and gave them to Abimelech, and the two of them made a covenant.*

The trade signified their entering into a covenant or agreement. There is no covenant without a trade.

If you have ever read natural legal documents, they seek to cover everything. They don't just leave things to be assumed or implied. They spell out in specifics what is being said. The same can be true in the spirit realm. The devil is a legalist. He will try to exploit us with things we didn't cover. So even though we know the trade is what resulted in a covenant, it is better to undo the covenant as well. We might say, "Well, once the trade that produced the covenant is undone, doesn't that take care of the covenant too?" Perhaps it does, but if the devil wants to make it an issue, it is better just to make sure the covenant is undone as well.

Isaiah chapter 28 and verse 15 speaks of the men of Jerusalem having made a covenant with death. They feel that because this covenant is in place, they will be protected from coming disasters.

> *Because you have said, "We have made a covenant with death, and with Sheol we are in agreement. When the overflowing scourge passes through, it will not come to us, for we have made lies our refuge, and under falsehood we have hidden ourselves."*

People in our ancestry made covenants with demonic powers to protect, provide for, prosper, and empower them. This is true in every culture and in every race of people. In the ancestry of every ethnicity there can be found covenants with demon powers. These covenants were made through sacrifice or trades. Quite often it was the sacrifice or trading of blood that made these covenants. Even the blood of humans was traded to enter into covenant with these demonic entities. Once these trades/sacrifices were made, the demonic powers then claimed the people as their own. According to what was dedicated to them when the trade was made, individuals, families, bloodlines, cities, nations, and whole cultures were given over. These covenants created by trading in the spirit realm are active until someone annuls them. Whatever the devil owns will eventually be destroyed through sickness, disease, poverty, and tragedy. This is why many people are sick today. Somewhere in their bloodline demonic powers have been given the right to own them. These rights have to be revoked. When they are, the demon forces lose the right to hold people in sickness.

We see this in the example of the woman who was bent over in infirmity for eighteen years. In Luke chapter 13, verses 10 through 17, we are shown Jesus dealing with something legal, then releasing healing:

> *Now He was teaching in one of the synagogues on the Sabbath. And behold, there was a woman who had a spirit of infirmity eighteen years, and was bent over and could in no way raise herself up. But when Jesus saw her, He called her to Him and said to her, "Woman, you are loosed from your infirmity." And He laid His hands on her, and immediately she was made straight, and glorified God. But the ruler of the synagogue answered with indignation, because Jesus had healed on the Sabbath; and he said to the crowd, "There are six days on which men ought to work; therefore come and be healed on them, and not on the Sabbath day." The Lord then answered him and said, "Hypocrite! Does not each one of you on the Sabbath*

*loose his ox or donkey from the stall, and lead it away
to water it? So ought not this woman, being a daughter of Abraham, whom satan has bound—think of
it—for eighteen years, be loosed from this bond on the
Sabbath?" And when He said these things, all His
adversaries were put to shame; and all the multitude
rejoiced for all the glorious things that were done by
Him.*

When the Bible says it was a *"spirit of infirmity,"* that means
there was a demonic power involved (Luke 13:11). Even Jesus said
that satan had bound her with this sickness. The word *bound* is
the Greek word *deo*. Among other definitions, it means "to be
put under obligation of law and duty." When Jesus loosed her, He
undid the legal right of satan to hold her and make her sick. This
woman had been in this condition for eighteen years because a
devilish power was holding her in it. I'm sure she had been prayed
for many times, yet still she stayed the same or had even gotten
worse. When Jesus sees her, He calls her to Him. He then does
two things. He "looses" her from the spirit of infirmity, and then
He touches her with His hand. As a result, she was healed. When
Jesus said, *"Woman, you are loosed from your infirmity,"* Jesus was
dealing with something legal in the spirit realm (Luke 13:12). The
word *loosed* is the Greek word *apoluo*, and it means several things.
Among other ideas, it means "to acquit one accused of a crime;
to set at liberty." By an accusation against this woman, satan had
a right to hold her in sickness for eighteen years. The idea here is
that Jesus pardoned, divorced, and dissolved a contract with satan
that gave him the legal right to keep her ill. The word *apoluo* also
means "to release a debtor" and "not to press one's claim against

another." Jesus, with His word, released this woman legally from the claim the devil had against her. He renounced every covenant and legal right the devil had to hold this woman in sickness. Once the covenant rights of satan were revoked, Jesus then laid His hands on her and released the anointing. The anointing was now free to have its effect because the legal covenant had been annulled. The result was that an eighteen-year infirmity was gone in seconds and/or minutes. This woman was healed.

The order of Jesus' steps is important. First, He removed the legal right that had been working against this woman. He then imparted the anointing through His touch. Jesus continued by explaining how this woman was healed. When the religious leader criticized Jesus for healing on the Sabbath, Jesus began to unveil the cruelty of the religious spirit. He pointed out that each Jew would untie their donkey or ox and lead it away to get a drink of water on the Sabbath. His first point was that these religious people, controlled by a religious spirit, cared more for their animals than they did this woman. The religious spirit is a very cruel thing. It masquerades as something from God yet has no heart for people. Then Jesus shows how this woman was healed. Just as someone would untie their animal and lead it away to get a drink, so Jesus did. With His word of *"Woman, you are loosed...,"* Jesus had untied her in the spirit from the legal right of the devil to hold her (Luke 13:12). With the touch of His hand, He had given her a drink of the anointing on His life. The anointing now had the right to bring healing because the legal rights of the devil had been revoked! When we understand this, it begins to make sense why some are not healed even though they appear to be dramatically touched by the anointing. The devil, it seems, actually has a right to deny the anointing its effect when there is still a legal right that has not been dealt with.

In my first book on the Courts of Heaven, *Operating in the Courts of Heaven*, I tell the story of a dear family friend who was diagnosed with breast cancer. I personally had prayed for this lady several times. Each time we would pray, she would have many sensations of the anointing touching the diseased part of her body. Intense fire and heat would come into these places. Pain would leave, and several other positive signs indicated that healing was taking place. Yet the disease continued to progress. It finally ended up in her lungs and another part of her body. In the midst of the battle, this woman would stand on the Word of God and believe for her healing. Nevertheless, her condition progressively worsened. It finally got to the point that she was taken home and placed in hospice care to simply await her death. I received a call from her husband to come to their home and pray once more. When I arrived, I was ushered into their bedroom. There were a couple of other ladies there praying. I entered the room and placed my hand on the head of this now emaciated person. She was unrecognizable from her state before this devilish disease attacked her. My heart broke for her and her condition. This lady was the mother of four children, the youngest being a daughter who was only thirteen. The heartbreaking thing beyond this woman's own personal struggle was that she too at thirteen had lost her mother to the identical cancer with which she was now being consumed. From the time I had known this woman, she had stood against the curse of cancer, saying that it wouldn't happen to her. Yet here it was about to take her out and cause her to leave her daughter of thirteen, just like her mother had left her. This fact had caused this woman to hang on longer than she would have otherwise. She didn't want to leave her children at forty-three years of age just like her mother had left her when she was forty-three. Clearly there was a family/generational curse operating that needed to be broken.

As I placed my hand on this woman's head one more time to pray, I felt an unmistakable passion of the Lord to heal. There was no way that it was the will of the Lord for this woman, wife, and mother to leave this world at this time. God's passion and desire was to heal her. As I felt this with such clarity, I prayed with as much unction as I could. I asked for God to heal her. I imparted one more time the healing anointing of the Lord into her diseased body. I mustered faith to believe for the impossible and see this woman restored and her life given back. I left the room hoping for the miraculous to occur. Yet no more than twelve hours later, this lady was dead and in the presence of the Lord. It hadn't worked. All that we stood for in believing that God healed had seemed to fail us. What had happened?

Later, I was to discover why, in my estimation, this woman was not healed. I found out first of all that she and her husband had directly gone against a prophetic warning. They had been told by two different prophetic voices not to associate with a certain minister because of dishonor. The prophetic warning had been that should they choose to do this, a demonic attack would come against their home. They had chosen to disregard this word and connect to this person while dishonoring another to whom they had sworn allegiance. They had become guilty of covenant breaking. This is a very serious thing in the spirit realm. Covenant breaking opens the door to demonic activity and grants it rights against us.

We see the severity of covenant breaking illustrated when Saul, the first king of Israel, broke a covenant made by Joshua with the Gibeonites. When Israel came across the Jordan in conquest of the land, the Gibeonites had deceived them. They made the Israelites think they were from a far country, when in fact they were inhabits of the land. They did this to prevent Joshua and the army he commanded from annihilating them. They asked to make a covenant with Joshua. Joshua did not inquire of the Lord and made a covenant with them. Joshua then discovered they had been tricked. Even though the covenant was made under falsehoods, Joshua and Israel were now committed to protect and defend these tricksters. They could not destroy them as had been commanded by God. Saul comes along several generations later and disregards this covenant. He kills some of the Gibeonites. In Second Samuel chapter 21 and verse 1 we see David dealing with a famine in the land. He asks God why this is happening, and God tells him it is because of a broken covenant.

Now there was a famine in the days of David for three years, year after year; and David inquired of the Lord. And the Lord answered, "It is because of Saul and his bloodthirsty house, because he killed the Gibeonites."

When David speaks with the Gibeonites, he discovers that in order to fix the broken covenant, they require seven descendants of Saul to be killed and hung. This seems atrocious, yet the devil was taking a legal right through the broken covenant to afflict a whole nation.

David had a quandary. How could he meet the requirement and not break covenant and walk in dishonor himself? David himself had sworn to Mephibosheth, the son of Jonathan, with whom David had a covenant, that he would provide and protect him always. David could not allow Mephibosheth to be one of the seven. If he did, then in his efforts to fix one covenant, he would break another. David saw to it that Mephibosheth was spared. Also, David could not dishonor Saul in this process. Even though Saul's activities had created this dilemma, he had still been the king of Israel and was anointed by God. David had refused to do him harm ever in any way. Even after Saul's death many years later, David walked in integrity by honoring him. He had to acknowledge that Saul had broken the covenant with the Gibeonites. This was necessary to fix it. Yet David could not and would not dishonor Saul in any way. To do this, David commanded that the bones of both Saul and his son Jonathan be retrieved. David then had them buried in their proper place in honor of both Saul, the first king, and Jonathan, David's friend through covenant. Second Samuel chapter 21, verses 12 through 14, tells us the effect of all this activity by David:

> *Then David went and took the bones of Saul, and the bones of Jonathan his son, from the men of Jabesh Gilead who had stolen them from the street of Beth Shan, where the Philistines had hung them up, after the Philistines had struck down Saul in Gilboa. So he brought up the bones of Saul and the bones of Jonathan his son from there; and they gathered the bones of those who had been hanged. They buried the bones of Saul and Jonathan his son in the country of Benjamin in Zelah, in the tomb of Kish his father. So*

*they performed all that the king commanded. And
after that God heeded the prayer for the land.*

David's methodical healing of a broken covenant without
destroying other covenants resulted in God heeding prayers for the
land. The famine ended and healing came to the land. Satan uses
broken covenants as legal rights to afflict things that need healing, whether it is lands, nations, or individuals. Once the legal
issues connected to sicknesses and diseases are dealt with, healing
can come.

I said there were two basic things that this woman and her husband had done that at least contributed to her not being healed.
The first was breaking covenant. The other was dishonoring and
seeking to steal away what belonged to another. After her death it
was discovered that her husband and perhaps she very deceitfully
and aggressively stole what another had entrusted to them. They
had been trusted explicitly with goods, finances, and power. With
this power, they secured loans from a bank and put up another's
house as collateral. It's a long story, but suffice it to say they got
money by giving someone else's property away over which they had
been granted stewardship. It was a very sinister and wicked thing
that was done. None of this was known while we were praying for
her healing. Micah chapter 2, verses 1 through 3, reveals what happened when authority is granted and then misused.

*Woe to those who devise iniquity, and work out evil on
their beds! At morning light they practice it, because
it is in the power of their hand. They covet fields and
take them by violence, also houses, and seize them.
So they oppress a man and his house, a man and his*

*inheritance. Therefore thus says the Lord: "Behold,
against this family I am devising disaster, rom which
you cannot remove your necks; nor shall you walk
haughtily, for this is an evil time."*

The result in this situation was exactly what the prophet
Micah spoke of. Because of their dishonor and thievery, a family
lost very much. If you were to know the whole story, not only were
finances and property lost that were never returned, but reputation
was destroyed as well. It was a very dastardly and wicked thing
done. Yet in the midst of this, there never was any acknowledgement
or repentance. Notice what the Scripture says will happen
to those who walk in this wickedness: a disaster will come from
which necks cannot be removed (see Micah 2:3). In other words,
there can be no deliverance unless there is repentance. In this case,
there never was. The woman died prematurely because of the legal
right of the devil to hold this sickness against her until she died.
Her neck could not be removed from this disaster, and neither was
her family's.

I want to be very clear. God did not kill this woman with
cancer. The devil took opportunity by the Word of God to build
a case against her. The devil was the one who killed her. He had
a legal right granted through covenant breaking, dishonor, and
abuse of power. There was a case against her in the spirit realm
that would not allow the anointing to have its designed effect. She
and her husband made an agreement with devilish powers when
they traded with them. This gave the devil the legal right to activate
the family curse she had been standing against for decades.
We must know how to undo every rebellion, trade, and covenant

made with demonic powers. The healing Jesus bought and paid for is now free to impact and restore our lives.

If any of this is relevant to you—if there is any guilt associated with something you have done against another or if someone in your bloodline has been guilty—there is a way to answer this case against you.

You should say, "Lord Jesus, I come repenting for any trade I have made with the devil and any covenant that has resulted. I humbly repent and asked for the blood of Jesus to annul this covenant. For any place my ancestors or I have gotten into agreement with demonic powers, I repent. Whether this came through sacrifice to demonic powers or activities of rebellion and sin, I repent. If I have not only made covenants with devils but have also broken covenants with man, I repent. I repent of any time I have been a covenant breaker, dishonoring or abusing authority. Lord, I ask that Your blood would now speak for me according to Hebrews chapter 12 and verse 24. I ask that Your blood would testify before the Courts of Heaven to annul every covenant with the powers of darkness. Lord, I ask for Your court now to set in place all that You did for me on the cross. Thank You, Lord Jesus, for securing my healing by Your atoning work."

"I now receive the effects of the anointing of the Holy Spirit into my body. Holy Spirit, come now to heal and restore any diseased part of my being. I ask, Lord Jesus, that any sickness operating against me now be judged as illegal from Your cross. I ask the Holy Spirit to touch me and make me whole. I receive everything You died for me to have. Thank You so much, Lord Jesus!"

By faith now receive the ministry of the Holy Spirit. He is the One who brings life and healing. We will see later how to move in agreement with the power of the Spirit fully. First we need to deal with any dedications in the spirit realm that are giving the devil legal access. Every case will be undone. Healing will flow like a river to you. Jesus has already secured it.

CHAPTER 6

DEDICATIONS REVOKED

Just like we must deal with rebellions, trades, and covenants, we must also revoke any and all dedications. Dedications are similar to covenants but can be different. Again, as in natural legal processes, it is good to cover as many bases as possible. We should seek to take away any and every loophole satan the legalist would seek to use. Dedications are simply places where something has been committed to satanic purposes. Dedications are actually the next progressive things from covenants. Once a trade has been made that secures a covenant, the result of the covenant can be a dedication. In other words, something is dedicated to satan as a result of the covenant made. This happens in bloodlines. Someone in our bloodline might have dedicated the forthcoming generations to devilish powers. The result of this is that the powers of darkness claim us. Ephesians chapter 2, verses 1 through 3, shows this:

> *And you He made alive, who were dead in tres-passes and sins, in which you once walked according to the course of this world, according to the prince of the power of the air, the spirit who now works in the sons of disobedience, among whom also we all once conducted ourselves in the lusts of our flesh, fulfilling the desires of the flesh and of the mind, and were by nature children of wrath, just as the others.*

Notice that we once walked according to the course of this world and according to the prince of the power of the air. This was because they claimed us and legally said they owned us. The result of this was the fulfilling of lustful ways and desires. In other words, the age and the powers of the air shaped us, influenced us, and con-trolled us. In the spirit realm, we were owned by something else. This can be the result of our bloodlines being dedicated to satanic powers in our history. This gives the demonic the legal right in the spirit realm to claim us.

My African friends tell me that every city in Africa has altars at the city gates. These altars are visible relics testifying that these cities have been dedicated to demonic powers. It is further under-stood that the inhabitants of these cities have their names on these altars. This causes the family lines of the people in these cities to be dedicated to these demonic powers. The powers of darkness therefore claim these bloodlines for themselves. Those who under-stand these things must get their "names" off these altars. In other words, in the spirit they must undo the dedication of themselves and their family line to satanic powers. Otherwise these powers of darkness will seek to "own" them and their bloodlines. When this happens, the devil is granted the legal right to operate against these family lines. Many times this results in sickness.

Lest we think this can happen only in Africa, we must know that every race, culture, and ethnicity has this operating against it. For instance, if you go far enough back in European culture, you will find cannibalism in operation—often in rituals whereby people would dedicate themselves to demons. Through the eating of human flesh they were devouring blood and making covenants and dedications to demons. These powers are still operating today. They look for any place a dedication was made in our bloodline as a legal right to afflict. As I said, all cultures have been dedicated to these devilish powers. Asian cultures have served and still serve "dead relatives." Polynesian cultures offered human blood sacrifices on altars to empower themselves. The Indian cultures of Central and South America apparently offered human sacrifices in the hundreds and even thousands.

I was in Machu Picchu in the jungles of Peru several years ago. These are the amazing ruins of the Indigenous people that still inhabit this region. While perusing this site, we came upon a place of sacrifice. It was clearly the place where not only animals were killed and offered, but also humans. There was a stone trough that was used to catch the blood of the sacrifice and gather it. When you realize what these sacrifices were for, it is quite a sobering thing. They were dedicating families, regions, and cultures to demonic powers. Demonic powers still try to claim these groups because of the dedications. They must be undone through the blood of Jesus in the Courts of Heaven.

We should point out that the Bible says that this was something of the past. According to Ephesians 2:1, Jesus has made us alive who were dead in this previous place. We by faith can sever any and every connection that would allow our dedication to satanic powers to operate. This includes sickness and disease and their operation against us. We should realize that just because someone prayed a prayer of salvation doesn't mean the conflict is over. In fact, when we yield our hearts to Jesus and ask Him to be our Lord and Savior, it is common for the devil to challenge this. He will stand up and seek to withstand this statement and build a case against us. This is especially true if we accept Jesus only as Savior and not as Lord! Making Jesus Savior is one thing in the spirit realm. Establishing Jesus as Lord is another. When we accept Him as Savior, we want the benefits of who He is and want He does. When we make Him our Lord, we are declaring His ownership over us. This can be a fundamental reason the devil is still claiming ownership over us as a result of some dedication in our history. We must experience not only His redemption, but also His Lordship. Otherwise, dedications in our ancestry still operate against us. Satan will claim a right of ownership and the right, therefore, to afflict with sickness. It is a good thing to make sure we do desire His Lordship as well as His salvation.

In our Western Christianity, this is a problem. Many have accepted Jesus to be their Savior, but there are so few who know little or anything about Him being Lord. I'm not really sure it is even valid to accept Jesus as Savior without also accepting Him as Lord. When the apostles spoke of salvation, they declared the need to confess Jesus as Lord. Romans chapter 10, verses 9 and 10, says clearly that there must be a declaration of Lordship for salvation to occur:

> *that if you confess with your mouth the Lord Jesus and believe in your heart that God has raised Him from the dead, you will be saved. For with the heart one believes unto righteousness, and with the mouth confession is made unto salvation.*

We must confess with our mouth the "Lord Jesus" and believe in our hearts His resurrection and we shall be saved! The word *saved* is the Greek word *sozo*. It means "to be protected, delivered, healed, and made whole." The word *salvation* in these verses is the Greek word *soteria*. It means "to rescue, to deliver, to produce health, and to save." When we confess Jesus as Lord and come under His ownership, the rights of the devil from any dedication are broken.

The word *confess* is the Greek word *homologeo*. It means "to say the same thing." In this passage, it means "to agree with what God has said about Jesus as Lord and the position He has given Him." It is a term that was used in a court of law. In that context, it meant "to agree with someone else's testimony in a court of law or to the terms of a contract in business," perhaps even "to consent to the terms of surrender in a war." This is what we are doing when we confess the "Lord Jesus." We are agreeing with God's testimony concerning Jesus. We are consenting that He is Lord. We are admitting and declaring that God has exalted Him above all others. This is what Philippians chapter 2, verses 9 through 11, indicates:

Therefore God also has highly exalted Him and given Him the name which is above every name, that at the name of Jesus every knee should bow, of those in heaven, and of those on earth, and of those under the earth, and that every tongue should confess that Jesus Christ is Lord, to the glory of God the Father.

We are before the Courts of Heaven, agreeing with the position God has granted Jesus because of His absolute obedience. He is the only One who has won the right to own us.

Notice that the word *confess* also means "to agree to the terms of a contract." In other words, we agree to all that is required of us. We also agree with what is required of God in this contract. In a contract, it is spelled out what is legally expected and demanded of each party. If a party does not fulfill what the contract declares, they are in danger of being sued. The contract is a legal document to be adhered to. When we confess the Lord Jesus Christ, we are not only agreeing to come under His authority, we are agreeing to what He has promised. When we make Jesus our Lord, we also get the benefits of His Lordship. These include His goodness, kindness, care, protection, and provisions.

David spoke of the benefits of God's Lordship in Psalm chapter 23 and verse 1: *"The Lord is my shepherd; I shall not want"* (Ps. 23:1). David proclaims that the Lord is his Shepherd. David understood what he was saying because he had worked as a shepherd caring for sheep. Being the shepherd of sheep is similar to being Lord. Not only does the shepherd care for the sheep, but he also has authority over the sheep by necessity. He cannot care for them if he has no authority over them. This is what makes Jesus such a wonderful Lord. He doesn't treat us as subjects to be used and abused. He treats us as prized people for whom He cares deeply.

Notice that David declared that as the Lord's sheep, he would not want. In other words, when David surrendered to the shepherding hand and authority of the Lord, his every need and desire was met. The condition of the sheep speaks of the care, heart, and ability of the shepherd. If the sheep are in poor condition, it is a reflection of the integrity and ability of the shepherd. If the sheep are healthy, nourished, and cared for, it reflects well upon the shepherd. The condition of the sheep is a shepherd's greatest testimony of how well he does his job. So it is with the Lord. Those who belong to Jesus and have come under His shepherding hand as Lord should reflect His goodness. The conditions of our lives testify of the character, intent, and kindness of Jesus as Shepherd.

In First Peter chapter 2, verses 24 and 25, we see a connection between healing and yielding to the shepherding and Lordship of Jesus:

> *Who Himself bore our sins in His own body on the tree, that we, having died to sins, might live for righteousness—by whose stripes you were healed. For you were like sheep going astray, but have now returned to the Shepherd and Overseer of your souls.*

Notice that Peter tells us the stripes of Jesus healed us. The beating He endured was what was required legally for us to be healed. Then he declares the reason this can work in our lives is because we have now returned and come under His authority. We have returned or come back to the Shepherd and Overseer of our souls. This activity allows what Jesus did on the cross to bring healing into our lives. When we are functionally under His authority, we get the benefits of all that He has done.

The problem is that so often we, in our rebellion, haven't come under His hand. We have accepted Him as Savior but not allowed His Lordship to operate in us. The devil therefore claims that we are still his because of previous dedications in our bloodlines. We must surrender to the Lordship of Jesus and yield to His authority.

The other legal meaning of this word *homologeo* is that we agree to the terms of surrender. When we make Jesus the Lord of our life and confess the "Lord Jesus," we surrender. We agree to His terms of surrender. This is where and when Jesus functionally becomes the Lord of our life. We are then placing into position His Lordship and removing the rights of the demonic to claim us because of prior dedications. Jesus spoke of this surrender in Luke chapter 14, verses 31 through 33. He talked of kings in battle and terms of surrender being discussed:

> *Or what king, going to make war against another king, does not sit down first and consider whether he is able with ten thousand to meet him who comes against him with twenty thousand? Or else, while the other is still a great way off, he sends a delegation and asks conditions of peace. So likewise, whoever of you does not forsake all that he has cannot be My disciple.*

In this passage, Jesus is declaring that the decision to surrender must be something that is considered carefully. There should be a counting of the cost. It shouldn't just be an emotional moment but a serious calculation. Notice the decision is made based on the perception of whether or not we can win the battle. Jesus says the king would ask for the conditions of peace. This word *peace* is the Greek word *eirene*, and it means "to be at one again." It also means "prosperity, quietness, and rest." The decision to surrender is weighed against what will be lost if we continue to resist and fight. It is also made considering what will be gained in surrender. We get the quietness, rest, prosperity, and oneness with the Lord and His forces. Jesus then tells us the terms of surrender and the conditions for this peace. We must forsake all and follow Him. When we are willing to do this, we can have everything from Him. The rights of any demonic power are revoked because we have surrendered ourselves to Jesus' Lordship and are His servants. In regard to sickness, the rights of the demonic to oppress us with disease are broken. The devil's right of ownership is revoked!

We see this picture in the case of David pursuing the Amalekites after they have attacked Ziklag. They have taken David and his men's families captive. They also have stolen their goods and possessions. As David pursues them in First Samuel chapter 30, verses 11 through 19, we see them coming upon an Egyptian servant of the Amalekites:

> *Then they found an Egyptian in the field, and brought him to David; and they gave him bread and he ate, and they let him drink water. And they gave him a piece of a cake of figs and two clusters of raisins. So when he had eaten, his strength came back to him; for he had eaten no bread nor drunk water for three days and three nights. Then David said to him, "To whom do you belong, and where are you from?"*
>
> *And he said, "I am a young man from Egypt, servant of an Amalekite; and my master left me behind,*

because three days ago I fell sick. We made an invasion of the southern area of the Cherethites, in the territory which belongs to Judah, and of the southern area of Caleb; and we burned Ziklag with fire."

And David said to him, "Can you take me down to this troop?"

So he said, "Swear to me by God that you will neither kill me nor deliver me into the hands of my master, and I will take you down to this troop."

And when he had brought him down, there they were, spread out over all the land, eating and drinking and dancing, because of all the great spoil which they had taken from the land of the Philistines and from the land of Judah. Then David attacked them from twilight until the evening of the next day. Not a man of them escaped, except four hundred young men who rode on camels and fled. So David recovered all that the Amalekites had carried away, and David rescued his two wives. And nothing of theirs was lacking, either small or great, sons or daughters, spoil or anything which they had taken from them; David recovered all.

David gathered necessary intel from this servant of the Amalekites. Notice that his owner and master had no more use for him once he fell sick. He left him to die. David and his men ministered to him and gave him food and drink. They restored his life and health. This happened because he agreed to "betray" his former master. He would not do it until David agreed not to turn him back over to his master and his cruelties, but he was willing forsake his previous master.

We too must be willing to forsake what we have previously served. We must realize that serving the previous master only brought us to sickness, disease, and desertion. We must come under the Lordship of a kind and good Master who loves us. This allows any dedications in our bloodline to devilish powers to be annulled and revoked. We can then come under the authority of another Master. Healing is free to flow into us because we now belong to the Lord. We are free from the torment of the previous master to whom we once belonged.

The Holy Spirit ministers Jesus and His Lordship functionally into place. Second Corinthians chapter 3, verses 17 and 18, declares the Lord to be that Spirit:

> *Now the Lord is the Spirit; and where the Spirit of the Lord is, there is liberty. But we all, with unveiled face, beholding as in a mirror the glory of the Lord, are being transformed into the same image from glory to glory, just as by the Spirit of the Lord.*

Clearly the Lordship of Jesus is functionally known through the power and person of the Holy Spirit. The Holy Spirit comes and takes over our life piece by piece and brings us under Jesus' Lordship. As we give room to the Spirit, this glorious process is known. This happens so that what we experience lines up with what we say. As time goes by, we are changed into the image and likeness of the One who created us. We are brought into liberty. This word *liberty* is the Greek word *eleutheros*, and it means "unrestrained as a citizen, as opposed to a slave." As we come under the

Lordship of Jesus through the Spirit, we come to unrestrained liberty as citizens of the Kingdom of God. Every restraint can come off of us, including sickness and disease. As citizens of the Kingdom, all the covenant rights and privileges are ours, including healing. The Bible makes a glorious statement in James chapter 4 and verse 5:

> *Or do you think that the Scripture says in vain, "The Spirit who dwells in us yearns jealously?"*

The Holy Spirit that lives in us yearns jealously for God's purposes to be fulfilled.

The Lord gave me a word several years ago. I heard Him say, "The Holy Spirit has come to possess all that the blood has bought." This means the Spirit is yearning jealously for God to have control over everything the blood of His Son paid for. In other words, Jesus' Lordship is to be recognized and seen functioning in our lives. All the devilish powers' claims of ownership are broken, and we belong absolutely to the Lord. He is worthy of this because of the price He paid. This is why the Scripture declares in First Corinthians chapter 6 and verse 20 that we were bought with an extremely high price:

> *For you were bought at a price; therefore glorify God in your body and in your spirit, which are God's.*

When we recognize the price Jesus paid for us, the desire to serve and glorify Him overtakes us. We realize He owns us. Every dedication of our bloodline to the devil is broken and revoked. He no longer owns us. We are the Lord's.

To bring this spiritual reality into place, here is a prayer we can pray:

Lord Jesus, we declare that we and our bloodlines belong to You. Any and every dedication made to the devil of our family line we now ask to be annulled by the blood of Jesus. We repent of any and every place we were dedicated to satanic powers through sacrifice. We ask these sacrifices to be annulled and the dedication rendered ineffective.

Lord Jesus, we also acknowledge Your Lordship. We say we agree with the testimony of God as Judge, the Holy Spirit as our legal aid, and all of Heaven that You are Lord. We now come under Your Lordship and declare that we belong to You. We are no longer our own; we are bought by the price of Your blood and sacrifice.

We also, Lord Jesus, invite the power of the Holy Spirit to exercise now Your Lordship in our lives. We agree that everything Your blood purchased the Holy Spirit will now possess. Every area of our lives we surrender to You.

We now declare that any and every right given to the powers of darkness through dedications to "own" us is now revoked. We belong only to the Lord Jesus Christ. Any and all sicknesses, diseases, and pains afflicting us because of this previous "ownership" is now revoked and removed! We receive the healing that is ours because of the offering of the blood and body of Jesus. We now exclusively belong to Jesus. No others have a claim on us. We are the Lord Jesus Christ's.

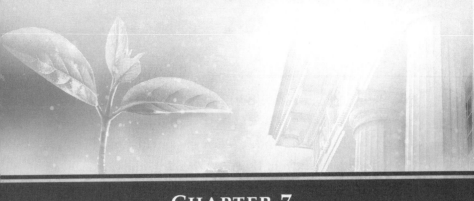

CHAPTER 7

THE NECESSITY OF FORGIVENESS

SEVERAL YEARS AGO WHEN I WAS LEADING A LOCAL work, we had a tremendous move of God's healing power. As a result of this, many people were showing up that did not attend our church but needed healing. They would come from close and far away because they had heard about people being healed. One Wednesday evening, we were having our mid-week service. As I was teaching during this time, I saw someone bring an older lady in a wheelchair into the building. My first thought as I was finishing up the teaching was that she was there to be healed. I have to say, this did not excite me. I was tired. I wanted to go home with my family as quickly as I could after the service. I knew if this woman needed healing, this was going to slow down my exit. This may sound cold, but it was the truth at the moment. I heard a man say years ago, "It is one thing to be tired in the work; it's another thing to be tired of the work." When you are tired "in" the work, all you need is a little rest. If you are tired "of" the work, you are on the edge of burnout, and this is more serious. At this moment I was just tired in the work. I needed a little time to be refreshed.

As I finished up the service, I began to talk with a few people as most exited the service. This lady, as I had suspected, was brought to me in her wheelchair. We greeted each other, and she began to tell me about her condition. She had a severe back injury that caused her to have to use this wheelchair. She was not paralyzed but severely incapacitated because of the pain from her lower back injury. She had to have the chair to function and move around. She was here to be prayed for and believe for her healing. As she sat in this chair, I laid my hand on the top of her head. The moment I did, I heard the Lord say, "I will do for this woman what I did for the man who was paralyzed and let down through the roof." I instantly understood what the Lord was saying. This story is found in Luke chapter 5, verses 18 through 26:

> *Then behold, men brought on a bed a man who was paralyzed, whom they sought to bring in and lay before Him. And when they could not find how they might bring him in, because of the crowd, they went up on the housetop and let him down with his bed through the tiling into the midst before Jesus.*
>
> *When He saw their faith, He said to him, "Man, your sins are forgiven you."*

And the scribes and the Pharisees began to reason, saying, "Who is this who speaks blasphemies? Who can forgive sins but God alone?"

But when Jesus perceived their thoughts, He answered and said to them, "Why are you reasoning in your hearts? Which is easier, to say, 'Your sins are forgiven you,' or to say, 'Rise up and walk'? But that you may know that the Son of Man has power on earth to forgive sins"—He said to the man who was paralyzed, "I say to you, arise, take up your bed, and go to your house."

Immediately he rose up before them, took up what he had been lying on, and departed to his own house, glorifying God. And they were all amazed, and they glorified God and were filled with fear, saying, "We have seen strange things today!" (Luke 5:18-26)

This story does not say that Jesus forgave the sin of unforgiveness. It just says He forgave the man's sin. It was his sin that was legally holding him in his sickness and paralysis. Before Jesus could heal this man, He had to first legally deal with the sin issue in his life. Of course, the religious leaders began to criticize Jesus in their hearts. They correctly understood that only God and those who God allowed to represent Him could forgive sins. For Jesus to forgive sins, He would have to be God. This was what Jesus was challenging them to understand. To prove that Jesus was in fact God, He declared the man forgiven, then healed him in the midst of them all. He dealt with the legal issue and then released the anointing. The result was that the man received his healing.

This is why they all departed glorifying God and speaking of the strange things they had seen.

The word *strange* in verse 26 is the Greek word *paradoxos*, and it means "something contrary to expectation." This is quite interesting. This word comes from two words: *para*, meaning "to come near," and *doxa*, meaning "glory." So, a paradox can be glory coming near. It challenges our thinking. It's not what we expected. Many times when we encounter the glory of God, it can seem paradoxical. It's not what we were looking for. It may even seem strange. Yet it is the glory of God being manifested to us. This is why we mustn't be too quick to judge or dismiss something as not being God. He can purposely show up in ways that we don't expect and challenge our preset conceptions of Him. We are called to judge and righteously evaluate things of the Spirit. Yet we must be careful that we do not allow our religious backgrounds and personal likes and dislikes to influence us too heavily. We could miss something with which God graciously wants to touch our lives.

Even though in this story it doesn't say this man's sin was unforgiveness, I "knew" the lady in the wheelchair had this issue in her life. This was stopping the healing of the Lord from operating in her life. Out of past experience, I knew that when you begin to delve into these kinds of things, it could be a long and drawn-out procedure. When you start searching out emotional issues of hurts and wounds, it can take a long time. Remember, I was tired and wanted to go home. So I chose to disregard what I was hearing. I knew that it likely would have been a lengthy thing to get into all of this. Instead, I just began to pray and release healing to her by faith. I declared the healing power of the Lord released into her back. As I had my hand on her head, I proclaimed all that

Jesus had done for her on the cross now released to her. I then took this lady's hand and told her to stand up out of the wheelchair. I pulled her toward myself as she stood up. She had gotten no more than a few inches out of the chair when I saw the grimace of pain on her face. She then began to cry out in pain. Clearly nothing had happened, and she was still very incapacitated.

At this point, I knew I really had no other option than to "delve" into this this realm concerning unforgiveness. To not be obedient to what I had heard the Lord say meant to allow this woman to go away in the same condition that she came in. I took a deep breath and dove in, fully expecting the process to take a significant amount of time. I asked her, "Ma'am, is there anything in your life that you think might be displeasing to the Lord?" This was a very generic question. Yet immediately she responded. She said, "My husband left me over twenty-five years ago with all our kids to care for and feed all by myself. I'm still mad about it." Wow! Talk about something being close to the surface. There was no digging necessary, no probing required. Bam! It was just there. I looked at her and said, "Ma'am, I understand your anger and pain. What he did was wrong. I don't know the circumstances surrounding his abandoning you, but there is no excuse for it. But it is your unforgiveness toward him that has you in this wheelchair. If you will forgive him, God will heal your back!"

At this point, there were tears streaming down her cheeks. The Spirit of the Lord was visibly dealing with her. I then addressed her a second time. I asked her, "Would you like to forgive him?" She responds that she would. I then led her in a prayer that went something like this: "Lord, I come before Your courts and before Your throne. I acknowledge You as the righteous Judge over all things. I first want to repent for my own unforgiveness. I repent for acting as judge over the sins of my former husband. That is not my place; that place belongs to You. He doesn't belong to me; he belongs to You. I give him to You. I ask You to forgive me for all the years I have had anger, bitterness, and even hatred in my heart toward him. I repent for every evil thought I have had against him and any time I have wished him harm. I say I want only good for him. Lord, please forgive me for the condition of my heart and my unforgiveness. I also now forgive my husband for anything and everything he did to me and my children. I release him from every judgment. I ask that the blessing of the Lord would come on him. I declare that he is not mine; he is Yours. Right now I forgive him in Jesus' name."

As she concluded repeating this prayer, I made a decree over her. This decree was similar to what Jesus did for the man He healed in the Scriptures to which we have referred. I said, "Based on your forgiveness and the cleansing of the blood of Jesus, I now proclaim you forgiven and freed from the sin of unforgiveness. The devil's right to hold you in this sickness and condition is now legally removed and revoked. I declare you forgiven." Some will ask why I would consider myself as having the authority to declare such a thing. The answer is found in John chapter 20, verses 22 and 23:

> *And when He had said this, He breathed on them, and said to them, "Receive the Holy Spirit. If you forgive the sins of any, they are forgiven them; if you retain the sins of any, they are retained."*

Jesus is prophetically proclaiming the coming of the Holy Spirit and the empowerment that will result. From this empowerment, the disciples/apostles will be able to walk as a representation of Jesus Himself. Based on the repentance of a person, they will be able to set in place the forgiveness of sins. The guilt, condemnation, regret, and effects of sin can be revoked and removed through this declaration. God will honor this from Heaven as we represent Him on the earth!

After this, I laid my hands on her head again. I prayed for all that Jesus had done on the cross to now touch her. I could sense the anointing of the Lord ministering to her. After praying a short prayer of declaration over her back condition, I took her hands again and began to help her stand up out of the wheelchair. To everyone's amazement, she stood up immediately. Her back condition of many years was instantly healed. She began to move with complete freedom—without any pain whatsoever. The last time I saw her, she was pushing the wheelchair in which she had come out the door of the sanctuary. God had healed this woman just like He healed the man let down through the roof. This occurred because this woman was willing to deal with the legal issue of unforgiveness. When she willingly repented for her years of unforgiveness, bitterness, and perhaps even hatred, the legal right of the devil was revoked. His right to hold her in this place of immobility was lost and removed! The case against her in the spirit realm was annulled and silenced! Again, we see that revoking the legal rights of the devil, our adversary, is at times critical to getting healed.

Unforgiveness is a huge sin that the devil uses legally against us in the Courts of Heaven. Jesus was very clear about this. He spoke of it several different times. Matthew chapter 6, verses 14 and 15, records Jesus teaching this principle. On the heels of teaching on prayer, He inserts this statement about forgiveness:

For if you forgive men their trespasses, your heavenly
Father will also forgive you. But if you do not forgive
men their trespasses, neither will your Father forgive
your trespasses.

Our forgiveness is connected to our forgiving others. When
we forgive others, we free the Father to forgive us. If we refuse to
forgive others for their offenses, we lose the right to be forgiven.
This is a very powerful statement. This should cause the fear of the
Lord to come upon us. My question is, if it takes forgiveness to be
saved, then if we refuse to forgive do we not have the promise of
eternal life and Heaven? I don't claim to have the answer to this.
I do know it isn't worth the risk. I definitely do not want to risk
not being saved and granted eternal life because I wouldn't forgive
another person. May the Lord help us to deal with our hearts and
to forgive. Our lack of forgiveness of someone else becomes a legal
right of the devil to deny us everything Jesus paid for us to have.

Matthew chapter 18, verses 21 through 35, records Jesus telling a parable about the need to forgive. It is quite revealing.

Then Peter came to Him and said, "Lord, how often
shall my brother sin against me, and I forgive him?
Up to seven times?"

Jesus said to him, "I do not say to you, up to seven times,
but up to seventy times seven. Therefore the kingdom
of heaven is like a certain king who wanted to settle
accounts with his servants. And when he had begun to
settle accounts, one was brought to him who owed him
ten thousand talents. But as he was not able to pay, his
master commanded that he be sold, with his wife and

children and all that he had, and that payment be made. The servant therefore fell down before him, saying, 'Master, have patience with me, and I will pay you all.' Then the master of that servant was moved with compassion, released him, and forgave him the debt.

"But that servant went out and found one of his fellow servants who owed him a hundred denarii; and he laid hands on him and took him by the throat, saying, 'Pay me what you owe!' So his fellow servant fell down at his feet and begged him, saying, 'Have patience with me, and I will pay you all.' And he would not, but went and threw him into prison till he should pay the debt. So when his fellow servants saw what had been done, they were very grieved, and came and told their master all that had been done. Then his master, after he had called him, said to him, 'You wicked servant! I forgave you all that debt because you begged me. Should you not also have had compassion on your fellow servant, just as I had pity on you?' And his master was angry, and delivered him to the torturers until he should pay all that was due to him.

"So My heavenly Father also will do to you if each of you, from his heart, does not forgive his brother his trespasses."

In response to Peter's question of how many times should someone be forgiven, Jesus tells this story. Maybe Peter's question was coming from a sincere heart. Maybe it was from a heart of looking for justification in a matter. Perhaps he had a problem with someone who kept committing the same transgression over and over again. He was tired of being used and abused in a situation. His question could have been from this perspective. In answer to this, Jesus tells this revealing parable. There are several key factors in this story about forgiveness. First, Jesus says we should forgive seventy times seven times. This would be 490 times. Jesus' point was not to keep a running tally of how many times we had forgiven. He was simply saying we must always practice forgiveness no matter what. We can never find a reason not to forgive. We cannot give ourselves license to carry anger, bitterness, and malice toward another person. This doesn't mean we have to be used by people. It is one thing to forgive; it is another thing to keep setting ourselves up for abuse. It is possible to forgive someone but not put ourselves in a place where they can harm us again. Walking in forgiveness and walking in wisdom are two different things.

Another lesson I see in this parable is that we must forgive from our heart. In other words, we can't just say we forgive while continuing to rehearse the offense in our minds and spirits. We must practice forgiveness until our hearts are changed. We must practice forgiveness until we only want good for those who have harmed us—until we do not secretly desire hurt or injury for them but instead truly desire that they and what belongs to them be blessed by the Father. Only the Lord can change our hearts, but we can position them for this supernatural occurrence.

Jesus also said that if we don't forgive, we will suffer the effects of the torturers (see Matt. 18:34). This is probably a reference to demonic powers that eventually begin to dominate our lives. Unforgiving people are the most miserable, bitter, and even unhealthy people you can meet. The refusal to forgive another person gives the devil the legal right to move against them. When someone is "given over" to the torturers, it means they now have a legal right to them. Again, to be unforgiving grants the devil the legal right to work against our lives. It stops us from being able to partake of everything Jesus died for us to have.

The last thing about this parable I will mention is that the forgiveness that had been granted was revoked. I don't completely understand this, but once the king heard of the brutality of the one whom he had forgiven, he revoked what had been granted to the servant. The once forgiven person was now judged and thrown into prison and given over to the torturers. This is a frightening thing. Perhaps among other lessons, this says that once we have received grace and forgiveness we are expected also to share it. This man's unwillingness to give to a fellow servant what the king had given him caused it to be lost! This may not fit some people's theology, but I don't believe Jesus spoke words that weren't important. If we choose not to forgive from the immense forgiveness we have received, our forgiveness can be lost.

I believe that this is what the Apostle Paul meant in Ephesians chapter 4 and verse 32 when he says the power to forgive is found in being forgiven:

And be kind to one another, tenderhearted, forgiving one another, even as God in Christ forgave you.

In other words, if I deny someone forgiveness, I am not giving the very thing I received from God. This is an insult to the grace of God. This is at least partially what Paul meant when he spoke of not receiving the grace of God in vain. In Second Corinthians chapter 6 and verse 1, we see the Apostle Paul urging the people of God to make full use of God's grace.

> *We then, as workers together with Him also plead with you not to receive the grace of God in vain.*

Part of receiving God's grace is being willing to use it to forgive others. When we have been forgiven, we are empowered to forgive others. If we choose not to do this, we can be receiving the grace of God in vain. I pray that we will learn to forgive from the nature of Christ that lives in us. We must get a deeper revelation of His love and forgiveness that will not allow us to withhold forgiveness from others. When we do, we deny the devil the legal right to use our unforgiveness against us.

The same grace that brings us healing also brings us forgiveness. James chapter 5, verses 14 and 15, shows us the connection between healing and forgiveness:

> *Is anyone among you sick? Let him call for the elders of the church, and let them pray over him, anointing him with oil in the name of the Lord. And the prayer of faith will save the sick, and the Lord will raise him up. And if he has committed sins, he will be forgiven.*

When the healing anointing is released, not only do people get healed, but the forgiveness of sin is also activated. This is because the same grace that brings healing also produces forgiveness. So, if I choose not to forgive, not only do I cut myself off from the forgiveness of the Lord, but I also detach myself from His healing grace. When I don't forgive, I cannot be healed. The devil has a legal right to use this against me to hold me in sickness.

Several years ago, I was ministering in the Memphis, Tennessee, area. I was there for three nights of healing meetings. We saw some amazing things happen in those meetings, including a young man healed of multiple sclerosis. He was so restored from his former condition that his boss actually contacted the pastor of the church. He reported what a wonderful testimony this once disease-ridden young man was to all around him. People were seeing the wonderful mercy of God through this young man and his healing. Many saw a perspective of God and His goodness that they had not seen before.

On the first night of these meetings, a lady came to me for prayer who was completely deaf in her right ear. She had not heard out of it for years. I began to pray and release the anointing into her ear. Even though I prayed very diligently, nothing happened. She remained completely deaf in that ear. She eventually went back to her seat, still deaf in her right ear. With a lack of anything else to tell her, I encouraged her to just continue believing through the course of the meetings. The meetings went very well the other nights, especially with the miracle of the young man with MS. When we came to the third and final night of the services, this same woman came forward again. She informed me that the Lord had spoken to her. He had reminded and instructed her that she needed to forgive her parents for times she felt they had injured her and done her wrong. She told me she had done this and asked if I would please pray for her again. I of course agreed to do this. I put my index finger in her ear and simply began to declare the anointing and healing power of Jesus into this deaf ear. Immediately, this woman began excitedly to declare, "It feels like warm oil streaming into my ear!" As this sensation continued in the lady's ear, her hearing began to return. Before the experience was over, the deafness in her ear had been removed. Her hearing had returned and was at full capacity. God had opened her deaf ear and restored her hearing. This happened because she forgave her parents and revoked the legal right of the devil to hold her in deafness. Her lack of forgiveness for her parents was the legal right the devil was using to deny what Jesus had provided for her at His cross. Once this right was revoked, the anointing was free to have the effect it is designed to have. She was healed. May we each forgive, remove the devil's case against us, and receive the healing that Jesus graciously provided for us from His cross. Great miracles await us!

This is a prayer that can be prayed to remove the legal rights of unforgiveness:

> *Lord, we lay our life down before You. Our life is not our own; we have been bought with a price. Lord, we acknowledge that we have held unforgiveness in our heart toward others. We repent of bitterness, anger, and even hatred. We ask, Lord, that You would create in us a clean heart and renew a right spirit in us. We need You to change our hearts. Right now, Lord, even as You have forgiven us, we forgive these. They belong to You. They are not ours. We put them into Your hands. We ask for blessing, life, success, health, and prosperity over them. Bless the works of their hands, and make them a success. We wish and desire only good for them. Thank You, Lord, for causing our heart to be acceptable to You.*

Lord, even as You have forgiven us, so now we forgive these. In Jesus' name. Amen.

CHAPTER 8

UNDOING
WORD CURSES

M Y WIFE, MARY, HAD A CHRONIC RESPIRATORY condition that she could not get rid of. She had even been to the doctor and had been prescribed medicine to help knock it out. Nothing was helping, though. We had a prophetic ministry that operates strongly in a seer capacity staying at our home. Because nothing else seemed to be helping, we decided by faith to step into the Courts of Heaven and see if anything legal was allowing this to function. As we began to pray, the seer began to "look" in the spirit and saw a well-known prophet standing at the Throne of God speaking evil of Mary. The seer said she could not tell what exactly the prophet was saying, but she knew it was critical and attacking. I knew this person that was being seen. I was somewhat confused by the fact that this person was speaking against Mary. I had no problem believing they would speak against me. In fact, in times past I had heard that they had done just that. I had gone into the Courts of Heaven and dealt with their words. The result had been curses and judgments removed and new realms of blessings released. Now this same person seemed to be attacking my wife in the spirit.

I contemplated for a few moments what the seer's revelation could mean. I suddenly remembered an encounter with this person. I was in a particular situation where I walked into a room full of ministers. Mary was with me on the trip but was coming behind me into the room. She had been held up for some reason. As I walked into the room, I was by myself. This person walked up to me and said, "Where's your wife?" They said it with a mocking and ridiculing sound and voice. I was somewhat taken aback by the tone of this question. The unsaid meaning of this question that I immediately discerned was, "She never stands with you. You're always by yourself. What's wrong with your relationship? Why doesn't she support you?" I answered the question that was asked and said, "She will be here in a moment. She had something she had to do." This person then said, "Oh" and walked away. This previous encounter with this person came to me when the seer said she saw a prophet standing at the Throne of God making accusations against Mary. I told Mary that it seemed this one was speaking critically against her and that their words and testimony from their criticalness could be causing this sickness.

Let me explain how this can happen. When someone with authority over our life or someone with authority in the spirit realm speaks evil of us, it can set things in motion. The place of authority they occupy makes their words even more significant. The demonic forces can take their words and build a case against us in the spirit realm. These words can give the devil the legal right to work against us and even afflict us with sickness. We were in no way "under" this person's authority who was criticizing Mary. They did, however, have a place of authority in the spirit realm. This place in the spirit allowed the devil to use their words more powerfully. I believe the devil and his forces take the words of people in authority and say before God's throne, "This one who is in authority or to whom You gave authority says this about this one." It is very similar to expert witnesses giving testimony in a natural court. Jurors and judges pay more attention to experts' and professionals' testimonies. They are considered "authorities" in the fields about which they are testifying. They are expected to know what they are talking about. Their testimony is given to support the facts of a case and to verify its truthfulness. Their testimony is designed to give credibility to the case being presented. People in authority are seen this way also before the Courts of Heaven. Their testimony can have more weight and power because of who they are. The devil loves it when people who have been granted authority speak evil against others. People who are in authority can be parents, employers, bosses, leaders, pastors, elders, husbands, and anyone who has a *position* that gives them authority. Their words can be used in the spirit realm to bless and/or curse. People who have authority are those who have been granted *influence* in the spirit realm. They may or may not have a position of authority. However, because of gift, office, visitation, call, and history with God, they carry authority in the spirit world. I believe these people must be extremely careful with their words. They can inadvertently bring trouble and hurt into people's lives. This is what this prophet was being used by the satanic to do against Mary. I'm sure they didn't even know it, but the devil was using their words to hold Mary legally in sickness.

The Apostle Paul understood this principle. He knew he was considered an "expert witness" in the Courts of Heaven. Therefore, in Second Corinthians chapter 10 and verse 8, he speaks of using his authority correctly:

> *For even if I should boast somewhat more about our authority, which the Lord gave us for edification and not for your destruction, I shall not be ashamed.*

Paul was aware that because of the place he occupied in the spirit realm, he had to be careful. His words had the power to build up and tear down. The greater the level of authority with which we have been trusted, the more measured we must become with our words. The devil is looking for the opportunity to seize upon our words and use them legally against us. Those who are in authority and/or carry authority in the spirit realm can unlock hindrances, harassments, sicknesses, and even tragedies against people. We must learn to bless and not curse (see Rom. 12:14). This is why those who walk in this dimension of authority must have the nature of Christ formed in them. This will allow them to properly use their authority.

As our prophet/seer friend shared what was legally allowing the devil to hold Mary in this sickness, we began to repent. Mary repented for any time she hadn't supported me. She repented for any time she hadn't involved herself in the ministry with me. I then declared before the Courts of Heaven as her husband that I was well pleased. I declared and gave testimony that I was happy with who she was and her level of involvement with me. With my testimony from my place of authority as her husband, I countered the other testimony. My testimony as her husband should have more weight than even the prophetic person's testimony. We also asked for the blood of Jesus that testifies to speak and undo these words and testimony of this prophet. We asked for their word to be annulled and for the Court of Heaven to no longer accept them. Once this was done and we had dealt with the legal rights, we then prayed for healing again for Mary. As a result, the chronic condition was healed. Wholeness was restored, and strength and power came again. The reason that prayer and medicine previously had no effect was that the prophet's testimony was being used against Mary. It had formed and allowed a word curse that had to be dissolved before healing could come.

I have had several situations like this. I also know of others. For instance, a minister friend of mine found himself in a very severe place of sickness. It was a very real threat of death that loomed over him. He testifies that were it not for his wife standing and not letting go, he literally would have died in the hospital. God revealed that the source of the sickness was a word curse against him. Let me explain. Ken had been healed of a severe heart condition in a meeting in which I was ministering. While declaring words of knowledge or perhaps apostolic decrees, Ken felt the power of God go into his chest. He shared that it was a force that knocked him backward. The result was that he was able to get off all medicines that had very strong adverse effects. He was healed, and his strength returned. Several years later, he was in the hospital with a different heart issue. As he progressively got worse, the Lord spoke to him and his wife. He began to know it was the people of God speaking against him that was causing this sickness. Their negative words toward him were working against him. This is what we call sometimes "charismatic witchcraft." God's people began to speak negative and critical words that the devil takes and builds a case with. This can allow the devil the right to devour.

Words have power because of who and what they empower! Proverbs chapter 18 and verse 21 tells us about the power of words:

> *Death and life are in the power of the tongue, and those who love it will eat its fruit.*

One of the reasons why words are so powerful is the spiritual forces that take advantage of them. They can use the words to build cases. Negative words can be used by the devil to build cases that bring death. Positive and right words can be used in the Courts of Heaven to bless and bring life. Remember that the accuser in Revelation chapter 12 and verse 11 is overcome by "the word of our testimony":

> *And they overcame him by the blood of the Lamb and by the word of their testimony, and they did not love their lives to the death.*

Not only is the blood of Jesus critical to overcoming the accuser, who builds cases against us, but the words we speak are also important. When we have the right testimony before the courts, we silence the accuser's case. If our words are wrong, they can empower his case. He takes our words as evidence and presents them to bolster his case against us. If people are speaking against us, those words can be used against us in the courts. This is what was happening to Ken. Enough people were speaking critical things against him and toward him. This was empowering devilish things seeking to take him out prematurely. As Ken and his wife had a revelation of the source of this deadly attack, they began to undo these words before God. As they did, Ken's condition began to improve. He was healed and continues to live a strong life today. If he hadn't recognized why this was occurring, he most likely would have died. It is sad, but many times it is the words of believers that are causing the problem. I believe we should regularly do "maintenance" in the spirit realm concerning any words being used against us. I try to keep the spirit realm purged of negative things lest the devil be empowered in his legal action against me.

There is one more incident where I saw word curses holding someone in sickness that I will mention. I was ministering in a church in the San Antonio, Texas, area. As I was praying for many that were sick, this one lady was incapacitated and unable to move freely. As best I remember, she wasn't paralyzed but was unable to breathe and move much. As I was releasing the anointing and praying for her, she began to get better. Yet I couldn't seem to get her completely freed and healed. A prophet leads the church in which I was ministering. As I continued to pray for her, he had a prophetic awareness that there was a word curse operating against her. He asked her, "Have you ever said the words, 'I wish I was dead'?" She acknowledged that she had. This prophet told her that her words had put a curse over her life. Her own words were being used to hold this sickness in place. I then led her in a prayer to annul these words and revoke their legal right to be used against her. I led her in a prayer of repentance for saying words that had empowered a spirit's right to hold her in this sickness. The prayer would have been something like this:

> *Lord, I surrender my life and lay it down before You. I repent for believing any and all lies of the devil. Forgive me, Lord, for every word I have spoken that the devil has taken and used as testimony against me. I repent for desiring to die when You gave me life. I humble my heart before You and ask for every word that has agreed with this spirit of death to be annulled. I ask for the blood of Jesus to speak for me and annul these words. I do not want to die. I want to live. Let the case against me now be removed and revoked. I receive my healing now!*

As soon as she had finished this prayer, I prayed and released the anointing again. Immediately, the healing power began to flow through her body. Her breathing became deep and unrestricted. She began to walk and then run around the room, completely freed. This happened because the word curse she had placed on herself was legally removed. Healing was free to flow into her!

As can be seen through these three illustrations, words give the devil the legal right to use sickness. There are times that in order to get healed, we must undo these words that have been spoken against us or perhaps even have spoken against ourselves. In addition to the prayer I previously described that I led this lady in, let me give you some biblical understanding of undoing word curses. In Isaiah chapter 54 and verse 17, we see the ability to "condemn tongues" that are speaking judgments against us. This verse declares that we can and should condemn every tongue speaking against us. It seems that the weapons formed against us are a result of the tongues speaking contrary to us. So, if we are to remove the weapons, we must silence the tongues. It is the tongues that are the driving problem. Once the tongues are revoked and removed, the weapons will vanish.

Of course, one of the weapons that can work against us is sickness. This is a picture of activity in a legal system. The word *judgment* in the Hebrew is *mishpat*, and it means "a verdict." So, words spoken against us can become sentences we are destined to live out unless we can stop them. There are two things that declare we have the right to do this. First, this is our heritage as the servants of the Lord. The word *heritage* in the Hebrew is *nachalah*, and it means "something inherited." It also means "occupancy." So, we have an inherited place in God by virtue of the new birth and the blood of Jesus. From this place in the spirit world, we have the right to condemn these tongues and words. The word *condemn* in the Hebrew is *rasha*, and it means "to declare as wrong." This position we have in God allows us to declare words that are against us as wrong. Furthermore, our righteousness, or right to stand in the judicial system of Heaven, is from the Lord. I believe the prophet Isaiah was seeing into the New Testament era and proclaiming the righteousness we now have by virtue of Jesus and His activities on our behalf. From this exalted place we can undo any and every word being used by the devil to level his weapon of sickness against us.

There are four steps I usually teach to undo words working against us. First of all, we must repent for every time we have spoken critically of others. Everyone is guilty of this on some level. We must acknowledge this and ask for the Lord's forgiveness.

The devil will resist us with our own sin. He will argue before the court that we cannot be forgiven of something we are also guilty of. We should also ask that any damage the devil has found a right to do to another because of our words be undone. We then should repent for any instance where what others have said about us could be true. Sometimes their words against us are based in reality. We must acknowledge this and repent. We should ask for the blood of Jesus to speak for us on our behalf. Thirdly, we can now ask for these words to be annulled so the devil has no legal right to use them. We can ask for the blood of Jesus to revoke and remove these words from record within the Court of Heaven. Once these words are annulled, the devil can no longer use them to build a case against us. Finally, we can declare that only what is written in the books of Heaven about us can happen (see Ps. 139:16). This includes the health we are to have. We can declare that any and every sickness connected to this word curse must now go. We should then ask for and receive the healing of the Lord into our bodies! When the devil is using words spoken about us to hold us in sickness, once they are revoked, healing will come. Let me give you a prayer to help undo words working against us.

> *Lord Jesus, I come laying my life down before You. As best I can, I lay my life down and present myself as a living sacrifice to You. I declare that I was made by You, through You, and for You. I declare I belong to You. I bring every word in the spirit realm that has been spoken about me before You. Any and every word that the devil is using that has been spoken by people, those in authority over my life, those who carry authority, or even me, I bring it before You. I first*

repent for every place I have spoken evil of others. I ask, Lord, to be forgiven because of Your blood that now speaks for me. I am sorry for all my negativity and words of destruction against others. I ask that these words would be annulled and that the devil be unable to use them to secure legal rights to harm others. I'm sorry for all of this. I also repent for anything that has been spoken of against me and anywhere there is truth in these things. Lord, please show me anywhere I am guilty of that which has been declared about me. I take responsibility for anywhere I am at fault or in sin. I ask that Your blood cleanse and forgive me and wash away any rights the devil might use. I now ask, Lord, that all words against me be annulled by the blood of Jesus. I ask for the speaking blood to speak on my behalf and revoke and remove all words that the devil could be using to build a case against me. Let these words be removed from the record of Heaven. Let every voice against me now be silenced. Let them not be used anymore to build any case against me. I further ask, Lord, that only what is written in my book of Heaven be allowed to speak before Your courts. Let only what is in my book in Heaven declare Your purposes concerning me. There is no sickness recorded in this book. Therefore, I ask that all sickness be removed from me. I ask for Your healing power to flow into me. I receive the healing touch of the Lord and walk in the divine health that is mine and recorded in my book. In Jesus' name. Amen!

CHAPTER 9

BREAKING ALL CONNECTION TO SICKNESS

ONCE YOU BECOME AWARE THAT THE DEVIL USES LEGAL rights to afflict with sickness, it can open a whole new way of thinking. When we know that it is God's irrevocable will for us to be healthy, so sickness is always of the devil, it changes our perspective. One of the things it should do is birth in us a lack of tolerance for any and all sickness. I am convinced that because we are not founded in this revelation, we live with disease we shouldn't. I have felt God's anger and disgust at sickness. I have tried to impart this to God's people. If they can ever feel what God feels about sickness, they will get healed. This will birth in them anger and a lack of tolerance toward sickness and disease. Otherwise, we tolerate things we should be aggressively using our faith to remove. When we recognize through revelation what Jesus did for us on the cross concerning healing and wholeness, sickness will be not allowed. We will take our place before Him and use what He did for us to remove it. If there is a legal right from which it is operating, we will take His sacrifice and revoke that right. We can then, with passion and a violent faith, receive the healing that is ours from Jesus. Many people do not get healed because they lack that violence of faith. This is not something we create. It is from the Spirit of the Lord. Yet we must posture ourselves before Him and receive the revelation that allows this violence of faith to be produced!

Even though my family and I have walked in divine health, we have had times when the enemy attacked. There is one more of these times I want to tell you about. This one is important because the devil found a legal right I knew nothing about. He exploited it, and Mary, my wife, found herself in the hospital desperately ill. I was preaching in Indianapolis, Indiana, on a Sunday morning. I was going home to Colorado Springs, where we lived, as soon as I was through. We were going to pack the moving trucks the next day and move back to Texas. We were going to base the ministry from the Dallas area. I was also to teach at Christ For The Nations as an adjunct professor in the third-year classes. We were all excited about this move. We sensed we were stepping into the next season of life and ministry. There had been several different prophetic people and ministries prophesy that the move to Texas was significant and strategic for what God had in store for us.

As I finished the ministry that morning in Indianapolis, I stepped off the platform. Immediately, my phone began to buzz. I looked at it, and it was from my home. This grabbed my attention because Mary was at home, but she never called. Plus I knew she knew I was ministering. I got to a place where I could answer the phone as the pastor finished the services. The moment I answered, my fears were confirmed. Mary was in intense pain. She was groaning and even crying out in pain. There is no more out-of-control feeling than to be several hours of flying time away when someone you love is in this kind of condition. I began to pray for her. Others that were there in the ministry prayed as well. I could not get her any relief. The pain kept increasing. Our daughter Hope lived close. I told Hope to get her mom to the hospital. She was in increasing measures of pain and trauma. I began my journey home, periodically checking on Mary. They admitted her to the hospital, administered drugs to her, and began to get her some relief. It was after midnight before I arrived because of delays. By the time I got there, she was sedated and not aware of much around her. This would begin a thirteen-day stay in the hospital. She was diagnosed with gall bladder issues and pancreatitis. They eventually took her gall bladder out and used different treatments to deal with the pancreas that wasn't working correctly.

During this time, I was staying at the hospital. Moving trucks were at our house loading them for the move back to Texas. Our house was sold, and we had to get out of it before the closing in a couple of days. I was trying to see after Mary, oversee the move at the house, and make all sorts of other arrangements. It was not a pleasant time. I would run over to where the moving was happening to take care of things and then go back to the hospital where one of our grown children was staying with Mary in her sedated state. We were able to get the trucks loaded and on the road to Texas. We were also able to get the closing on the house done. The real estate agents brought the paperwork to the hospital. Mary and I signed it, convincing them Mary was coherent enough to do so. By law you must be in a right state of mind to sign these documents. Mary later said that she has no remembrance of this. Oh well! In the middle of all this, the doctors were trying to get Mary stable enough for surgery to take the gall bladder out. They sought to reduce the infection that had developed so the surgery could be done.

In the midst of this, I had a dream. I was wondering, why is this happening? Why at this time? What would be allowing this in the spirit realm? Is this an attack on us right now because we are moving into the season that has been prophesied? What is going on? The dream began to bring some understanding so I knew what to deal with in the Courts of Heaven. This was definitely a case for the courts.

In the dream, there was a woman who came up behind me and wrapped her arms around me. She then began to squeeze me with what I understood to be supernatural strength. I knew her intentions were to squeeze the life out of me. I knew I was in a life-and-death struggle with her. By the way, later when I told Mary about this, she said this is what she felt like was happening to her. She said it was as if the life was being squeezed out of her. I was able to take my right arm and maneuver it in between her arms and my body. When I did this, I was able, with supernatural strength, to press her arms out and break her hold (breaking her hold is significant). I then walked over and sat down on a couch that was in the room. This woman walked over and sat down beside me. She then handed me a check for one thousand dollars. The thought that ran through my mind in the dream was, "Maybe she's not as bad as she seems." The dream then ended. As I contemplated the dream, I knew this woman represented the Jezebel spirit. In Colorado Springs, one of the ruling spirits in that region, in my opinion, is Jezebel. The spirit of Jezebel hates the prophetic and apostolic. Remember she was one who persecuted and intended to kill Elijah. She was the wife of King Ahab, king of Israel. From this position she brought all sorts of idolatrous and demonic worship into Israel. Even though the original woman Jezebel is dead, the spirit she represents is very much alive. There is hatred against the apostles and prophets of the Lord. They are a tremendous threat against her and her agenda. She will therefore do everything in her power to remove them. If you live in Colorado Springs, Colorado, as beautiful as this city is in the natural, this spirit is one that desires to influence.

Mary and I had a small apostolic work in this city. We had started it as a base to minister in and from. We were not the pastors of it but the apostolic leaders. There were others I had on staff that pastored and took care of the people. There was this one family who came to me early on in the process of building this house. They began to declare how excited they were about what God would do apostolically in their city through this work. They then gave five hundred dollars to us to "honor" our apostolic place. They later gave another five hundred dollars. This was the one thousand dollars I saw in the dream. From the time I met this family, I had a sense that something wasn't right. I suspected they were under the influence of Jezebel. Even though their words were glowing and exciting, I felt they wanted control and undue influence. I received the one thousand dollars and indeed did think, "Maybe I'm wrong about them." I wasn't. It began to become apparent that their motives were not pure. They had a real problem with my operating in apostolic authority. They caused great damage in the work as we moved forward.

Here was the problem. When I received the one thousand dollars from them, this created a "connection" with this Jezebel spirit—not just the one operating through these people, but that which influenced and even ruled the city. The people I received the money from were "influenced" by and therefore represented this Jezebel spirit in Colorado Springs. They didn't know this and probably would vehemently deny it. The money they gave me, however, made a connection in the spirit world to Jezebel. In actuality, a trade was made that made a connection and even formed some level of covenant. Remember we talked about trades in chapter 4. When I received the money from that spirit, it was able to say, "Because you have taken something from me, I can now take something from you." This is a trade. It took my wife's health away in the most damaging time it could. If I was going to get Mary well, I was going to have to break this connection created by the money and undo this trade! I had to get the rights of this Jezebel spirit revoked so that God's healing presence could make Mary well.

Mary was basically sedated and incoherent at this time. In this state, however, I had her pray with me and agree. As we prayed, I began to deal with things in the spirit realm that had occurred when I received this money. Let me say here that we can receive money, but we need to learn how to cleanse it in the spirit realm.

I will show how to do this later. Money can and does carry what it has been dedicated to. In offerings in church services, it is a very good practice to cleanse the offering and ask God to burn up anything impure in it. Spirits seek to get their clutches in ministry through offerings brought with impure motives. Even paychecks from companies should be cleansed. Sometimes companies are dedicated to demonic powers. It's not that believers can't work for them. Paul actually said that if we are going to be that stringent, we are going to have to just go on to Heaven. First Corinthians chapter 5, verses 9 and 10, tells us that we can't get away from all this while living in the world. The fact is, we shouldn't even want to.

I wrote to you in my epistle not to keep company with sexually immoral people. Yet I certainly did not mean with the sexually immoral people of this world, or with the covetous, or extortioners, or idolaters, since then you would need to go out of the world.

Paul said if we are going to shun everything that is immoral, demonic, and godless, we have to leave the world. This is why I ignore so many calls to boycott something. One of the biggest is Starbucks Coffee. I realize they are committed to demonic powers. When I drink a Starbucks, I simply sanctify it to the Lord.

Paul further addressed this in Romans chapter 14, verses 4 through 6:

Who are you to judge another's servant? To his own master he stands or falls. Indeed, he will be made to stand, for God is able to make him stand. One person esteems one day above another; another esteems every day alike. Let each be fully convinced in his own mind. He who observes the day, observes it to the Lord; and he who does not observe the day, to the Lord he does not observe it. He who eats, eats to the Lord, for he gives God thanks; and he who does not eat, to the Lord he does not eat, and gives God thanks.

Paul said, *"Let* [everyone] *be fully convinced in his own mind"* (Rom. 4:6). He is also declaring that we should stop judging each other. There are those who don't eat because of conviction, and there are those who do eat and give thanks to God. When we are able to thank God for the pleasure we are deriving from something, it is acceptable to Him.

I have ministered quite a bit in Japan. In Japan, there are believers who work for companies dedicated completely to demonic powers. These people do not quit their jobs. They will not take oaths to these powers, and they cleanse their paychecks when they receive them so that they are not in connection or covenant with these demons. They would have to go out of the world if they adopted the viewpoint of some believers. When we know how to deal with these things, "greater is He that is in us than he that is in the world" (see 1 John 4:4). We have authority to deal with these issues in the unseen realm so that demons cannot take advantage of and seek to claim us. Paul would even later say that for those of us who have knowledge, everything is permissible. Paul addresses this in First Corinthians chapter 8, verses 4 through 8:

Therefore concerning the eating of things offered to idols, we know that an idol is nothing in the world, and that there is no other God but one. For even if there are so-called gods, whether in heaven or on earth.

Paul declared that when we have knowledge of who the one true real God is, we are free. We can eat, drink, enjoy, and give honor to the Lord who made everything. Paul said it is the knowledge we "eat" it with that is important. If we eat in faith toward the Lord, then we can enjoy it and give honor to Him. If we, from revelation, esteem all things having been created and coming from God, we can then enjoy them as from the Lord. However, if we have a weak conscience—in other words, we don't have revelation of these things—we can be defiled. Paul says all of this is a personal issue. We are not to condemn where someone is in their walk with the Lord. We are not to chastise people for their revelation level. Let me be clear that this is not justifying immoral, unethical, illegal, or unscriptural behavior. This is dealing with added requirements to the standard of God.

Paul had an understanding that we are free when we are living under the constraints of the Spirit of the Lord. Galatians chapter 5, verses 16 through 18, shows us Paul's efforts to bring us into liberty:

> *I say then: Walk in the Spirit, and you shall not fulfill the lust of the flesh. For the flesh lusts against the Spirit, and the Spirit against the flesh; and these are contrary to one another, so that you do not do the things that you wish. But if you are led by the Spirit, you are not under the law.*

When we walk in the Spirit, we are empowered to refrain from fulfilling the lust of the flesh. Also, when we are led by the Spirit, we are free from the mandates of the law. As believers, we must know that we are not to be rule-keepers but to live under the control of the Holy Spirit. This is where our fulfilled righteous comes from (see Rom. 8:5). This is the liberty Paul fought to see the Church come into under the New Covenant.

Having said all of this, I believe it is healthy to "cleanse" all money that might have been dedicated to devilish purposes. This is what I had to do to break the spirit of Jezebel that was attacking my wife. When I did this and broke that power by removing its legal right, Mary began to get well. The healing of God came, and Jesus' touch brought restoration. However, the connection with Jezebel that allowed the attack had to first be revoked. To "cleanse" money, this is a good prayer to pray:

> *Lord Jesus, I come laying my life down before You. I declare You are my God, my King, and my Lord. I honor You with my life. I declare to You that You are my source and my provider. I repent of any trust I have in anything or anyone but You. I clearly say, "I am Yours, and You are my source and complete sufficiency." Lord, I bring all the money that has come into my life, whether earned, given, donated, found, or secured through any other means. Any wrong motive, dedication, spirit, or connection to this money I ask to be removed. I ask that the fire of Heaven would burn up and consume anything attached to it that would seek to make a connection to control, hurt, or enslave*

my family or me. I ask by the blood of Jesus that any-
thing devilish attached to this money be annulled and
revoked. I cleanse this money now to Your purposes
and desire. This money is now sanctified for Your use
in meeting our needs and advancing Your Kingdom.
In Jesus' name. Amen.

If there is sickness involved in your life or the life of someone else that you suspect is connected to this money, the following is a good prayer to pray:

Lord Jesus, I come before You now and ask that any
sickness taking advantage of a devilish connection
because of money be removed. Lord I ask that as the
money is now sanctified and this connection is broken,
healing now come to the body. Let sickness and disease
be removed, its power destroyed, and the healing flow
of Jesus now touch this life. I rebuke the power of the
enemy and say that it must go this instant! In Jesus'
name, your authority is removed and your rights to
operate are revoked. In Jesus' name, you must now
leave! Healing now flows into this body, and resto-
ration now comes completely! In Jesus' name. Amen.

We must move in complete authority and power. Once the legal rights have been revoked, healing is now free to come. We shall live and not die and declare the glory of the Lord (see Ps. 118:17). In the next chapter, we shall learn how to discern the dev-il's operation and release the anointing.

CHAPTER 10

UNDERSTANDING THE DEVIL'S LEGAL AND ILLEGAL PLACE IN THE SPIRIT

LONG BEFORE I KNEW ANYTHING ABOUT THE COURTS OF Heaven and the legal dimension of the Spirit, we saw people healed. By taking our authority in the spirit and releasing the anointing, we saw many people delivered and healed of sicknesses. As I have said though, there were others who weren't healed. The Lord would visibly touch many of these by His Spirit, yet they still remained sick. The truth is, some even died prematurely. As mentioned earlier, this was the word that the Lord spoke to Mary, my wife: "If you do not pray for them correctly, they will die." I now know this was a reference to understanding the Courts of Heaven and removing the legal rights of the devil. I do not, however, want to leave the idea that everything is about the Courts of Heaven when it comes to healing. My own experience and the teaching of others clearly show this isn't true. There are times when all that is necessary for people to get healed is the anointing mixed with faith. In fact, this is true for probably the majority of the miracles Jesus performed. People simply came to Jesus in faith, and the anointing and power in His life healed them. However, there are times when this doesn't seem to be enough. This is where I believe the Courts of Heaven come in. From the Courts of Heaven, we remove and revoke any legal right of the devil so that people can experience the healing Jesus died for them to have.

Based on this explanation, it appears that the devil operates from both a legal and an illegal position. We know from previous study that the devil is the adversary—*antidikos* in the Greek. This is found in First Peter chapter 5 and verse 8:

> *Be sober, be vigilant; because your adversary the devil walks about like a roaring lion, seeking whom he may devour.*

Remember the word *antidikos* means "one who brings a lawsuit." Therefore, this speaks of a position in a legal system. The devil searches for a legal right to devour us. Someone who brings a lawsuit must first have built a case. We have discussed several things in the Scriptures that can enable these cases to be built that would then allow or cause sickness. If satan is operating from a legal place, we must them remove that legal place through the blood of Jesus.

Another reference that shows the legal nature of the devil is Revelation chapter 12, verses 10 and 11:

> *Then I heard a loud voice saying in heaven, "Now salvation, and strength, and the kingdom of our God, and the power of His Christ have come, for the accuser of our brethren, who accused them before our God day and night, has been cast down. And they overcame him by the blood of the Lamb and by the word of their testimony, and they did not love their lives to the death.*

The word *accuser* here is the Greek word *kategoros*, and it means "one against you in an assembly; a complainant at law." The accuser of the brethren is not someone in the natural speaking evil of you. The accuser of the brethren is the devil, who is before God day and night bringing legal accusations against us. He is speaking in the spiritual realm, or the Courts of Heaven, against us. He is bringing railing accusations to deny us all Jesus died for us to have. Clearly from Scripture, healing is a covenant right in both the Old and New Testament. Even Jesus said concerning the woman bent over for eighteen years that she should be healed. She had a covenant right as being in the Abrahamic covenant to healing. He says in Luke chapter 13 and verse 16 that this woman had a right to healing because of the Abrahamic covenant:

"...So ought not this woman, being a daughter of Abraham, whom Satan has bound—think of it— for eighteen years, be loosed from this bond on the Sabbath?."

When Jesus spoke the word and dealt with the legal issue holding her from healing, she was immediately healed. Jesus loosed her from the contract in the spirit that the devil was using to hold her in sickness. Amazingly, she was healed.

We have spent the majority of this book dealing with undoing the legal rights of the devil to hold people in sickness. Having said this though, the devil also works from an illegal position. I know we have already discussed this, but I want us to get this into our spirit. If the devil is using something legal, it will have to be undone for healing. If he is just operating as a bully or, as the Bible declares, as *"a thief and a robber,"* this is illegal (John 10:1). In John chapter 10, Jesus shows us the nature of the devil:

> *Most assuredly, I say to you, he who does not enter the sheepfold by the door, but climbs up some other way, the same is a thief and a robber.*
>
> *The thief does not come except to steal, and to kill, and to destroy. I have come that they may have life, and that they may have it more abundantly.*

The devil is the thief and a robber who comes to steal, kill, and destroy. This means he doesn't only do things legally; he also operates from an illegal position. If satan is doing something legally, we must discern what he is using and remove it. If, however, he is doing something illegally, we must simply take the anointing, authority, and power of the Lord and break its effect. A property attorney explained it to me this way: There is a difference between an eviction and a trespass. You have to take someone to court to get an eviction. They have a right based on a contract that is in force. You cannot simply kick them out. They have a legal document that says they can live in and on the premises. To remove them, the legal rights they are using have to be revoked. Then they can be removed. A trespasser, however, has no legal rights. You can call the police and have the person thrown out of the property. They don't have a contract. This is a powerful illustration of what I'm seeking to communicate. If the devil has something legal he is using to torment with sickness, to get people healed we must revoke the legal rights he has. He can then be evicted! Healing will come. If, however, he is simply trespassing, no court activity is required. We simply take the anointing and authority of the Spirit of God and kick him out and see healing come.

As I mentioned earlier, if there is a legal right, it can even stop the anointing from having an effect. I have watched people be touched powerfully by the anointing and even the glory, and they still were sick. This is because the legal rights of satan have not been removed. However, once the legal rights are revoked, or if satan is just operating as a thief, we must know how to function in the anointing. The anointing is what breaks and destroys the yokes. In the remainder of this chapter, I want to bring understanding concerning the anointing. If we don't know how to function in the anointing, we can remove and revoke all legal rights and not see people healed. It is the anointing that brings the healing life of God.

My wife likes to shop online and on home shopping networks on television. She really likes QVC. This is the premier home shopping channel on television. I know she does this because there are packages being delivered to our home regularly. When I come home from my travels and ministry, I find packages in the mailbox, at the front door, inside the house, and on the counter in the kitchen. Most of these have been ordered online or off television. I use this to illustrate the anointing and the Holy Spirit's ministry.

Let me explain. When my wife sees something she wants on television, she calls the number onscreen. The people answer, and she tells them what she wants. She places her order. They then run our credit card to pay for these items. The moment the credit card transaction occurs, we "own" these items. We own them, but we haven't possessed them. The people at the home shopping network then communicate with the warehouse, secure the items purchased, package them up, put them on a truck, ship them to the airport, fly them to our area, take them from the plane, eventually place them on another truck, and deliver them to our house. The items we purchased and have owned for several days we now possess! For us to receive and possess them, there was a delivery system to get them into our hands. This is very much what happens in the spirit realm. When Jesus died on the cross, He purchased and paid the price for our healing! If we are to receive what has already been purchased, we must understand the delivery system. The Holy Spirit is the delivery system of God. He takes everything Jesus paid for on the cross and delivers it into our lives. We must know how to cooperate with the Spirit or we cannot get what has already been paid for. We cannot be ignorant of spiritual things. We must understand the ways of the Holy Spirit or we will not get the benefits of who He is. The Apostle Paul wrote in First Corinthians chapter 12 and verse 1 that we should not be ignorant of spiritual things and how the Spirit operates:

> *Now concerning spiritual gifts, brethren, I do not want you to be ignorant.*

Paul was instructing this church in how to move with and flow in the things of the Spirit. He then begins to outline nine spiritual manifestations of the Holy Spirit. This was his effort to help them understand "some" of the realms that the Spirit could reveal Jesus in and through. The more we can understand and cooperate with the Spirit, the more power and anointing that will produce healings and breakthroughs.

Let me give five secrets to cooperating with the Holy Spirit as God's delivery system of everything Jesus died for us to have. First of all, we should reverence and respect the Holy Spirit. When I say the Holy Spirit is the delivery system, in no way am I minimizing who He is. I am simply seeking to communicate His function in God's heart for us. If we are to be able to receive from Him, we should always treat Him with great reverence, respect, awe, and admiration. He is God. One of the sins against the Spirit is to "insult" Him. Hebrews chapter 10 and verse 29 speaks of insulting the Spirit of grace:

> *Of how much worse punishment, do you suppose, will he be thought worthy who has trampled the Son of God underfoot, counted the blood of the covenant by*

which he was sanctified a common thing, and insulted
the Spirit of grace?

This is a pretty scary Scripture. I point it out to show simply
that the Spirit of God can be insulted. We are always to treat Him
with great respect.

Several years ago, I was very close to a very strong ministry.
Great miracles were the norm in this ministry. During one set of
meetings, the minister prayed for all the pastors that were there.
I had been prayed for and imparted to many times by this man.
This time, as he prayed for me before the thousands that were
there, the Spirit of God touched me so powerfully that I literally
went flying through the air. Those who were behind me, suppos-
edly for the purpose of catching me, were taken out. I was like
a bowling ball being hurled through the air. Everyone—either
by the anointing or the force of my body—went flying themselves. It was a very powerful and life-altering experience. After
the service was over, I was going to ride the bus back to our city
that a number of our church people had come on. By the time
I got to the bus, our group was already onboard. As I boarded
the bus, the people began to laugh and carry on about what had
happened to me. Most were just laughing in good fun. One of
the chief people with the ministry we had just attended had
followed me to the bus just to say hello to everyone. He heard
everyone laughing at what had happened to me. He stepped onto
the bus and began to upbraid and chasten everyone for their attitude toward what had happened. This was the standard of this
ministry. They treated the Holy Spirit and what He did with
great respect. This man was offended by the lack of reverence

being shown toward the power of the Spirit of God. Everyone went extremely quiet as a conviction settled over us concerning our flippancy toward the things of God. I have learned that we must treat the Holy Spirit with the reverence due to Him. The more we will reverence and respect Him, the more He will manifest in our lives. I worry there isn't enough fear of God in the Church today. Lord, forgive us for not honoring and esteeming You the way we should.

Another thing we must do is worship Jesus. The Holy Spirit is here to manifest and reveal Jesus. Jesus actually said that the Spirit would not speak of Himself but would glorify Jesus. John chapter 16, verses 13 and 14, declares the Holy Spirit is here to magnify Jesus:

> *However, when He, the Spirit of truth, has come, He will guide you into all truth; for He will not speak on His own authority, but whatever He hears He will speak; and He will tell you things to come. He will glorify Me, for He will take of what is Mine and declare it to you.*

The purpose of the Holy Spirit is to lift up Jesus. Anywhere there is a people magnifying Jesus the Spirit of God will come. His passion is to glorify Jesus. If we want the power, presence, and person of the Spirit among us, then begin to give glory to Jesus.

In John chapter 7, verses 37 through 39, we see Jesus crying out. He is calling for the thirsty:

> *On the last day, that great day of the feast, Jesus stood and cried out, saying, "If anyone thirsts, let him*

come to Me and drink. He who believes in Me, as the Scripture has said, out of his heart will flow rivers of living water." But this He spoke concerning the Spirit, whom those believing in Him would receive; for the Holy Spirit was not yet given, because Jesus was not yet glorified.

Jesus was speaking about the Spirit. It says the Spirit *"was not yet given, because Jesus was not yet glorified"* (John 7:39). I realize this is referring to Jesus' death, burial, resurrection, and ascension. Yet there is a principle also at work here. The Holy Spirit comes only when Jesus is being glorified. If you want the power and glory of the Holy Spirit, then begin to glorify Jesus. In particular, our worship and adoration of who He is will release the power and presence of the Lord among us. It will result in rivers of living water beginning to flow. Notice it isn't just a river, but rivers, that start to flow. This is a result of the Spirit responding to the glorifying of Jesus!

Another thing to move and cooperate with the Holy Spirit is the realm of faith. Faith is what attaches us to the power of the Holy Spirit. I liken it to an electrical outlet in a house into which lamps, appliances, and other items can be plugged. The electrical current behind the outlet allows these to operate and provide service and convenience to us. Electricity is an unseen source and yet very powerful. It brings life to otherwise motionless things. This is very much like the Holy Spirit. He is unseen and yet powerful as well. When we connect with Him, life begins to flow. Resurrected power is released when we are joined to Him. The key is to connect. The power connected to a wall outlet does no one any good unless something is plugged into it. There has to be a purposeful act of connecting to the power that is unseen yet available. We connect and plug into the power of the Holy Spirit through faith. With all the teaching on faith, it seems that we still struggle to get it. Yet without faith we can have the most powerful anointing present and completely miss what is available to us.

This is what happened to the people in Nazareth, where Jesus grew up. Their familiarity with Him caused them to miss what He was carrying. Their unbelief would not let them plug into the power of the Holy Spirit in which He moved. Mark chapter 6, verses 5 and 6, tells us that Jesus marveled at their unbelief:

> *Now He could do no mighty work there, except that He laid His hands on a few sick people and healed them. And He marveled because of their unbelief. Then He went about the villages in a circuit, teaching.*

Their unbelief would not allow them to connect with the anointing and power that was present among them. Many times people do not get healed, not because something legal is resisting them, but because of the unbelief attached to our humanity.

I believe this is one of the reasons the Holy Spirit has come. He wars with our unbelief and seeks to bring us into legitimate faith. John chapter 16, verses 8 and 9, tells us the Holy Spirit will convince us of unbelief. I believe this means that He will contend with our unbelief to bring us into places of powerful faith.

And when He has come, He will convict the world
of sin, and of righteousness, and of judgment: of sin,
because they do not believe in Me.

Notice that unbelief is considered a sin. We tend to excuse our unbelief and make room for it in our life. If we find in our lives unbelief that will not allow us to connect and plug into the power of the Spirit, we must deal with it ruthlessly. We must acknowledge it and repent for its connection to us. Hebrews chapter 3 and verse 12 calls unbelief an evil thing:

Beware, brethren, lest there be in any of you an evil
heart of unbelief in departing from the living God.

Departing from the living God doesn't mean we leave Him or even backslide from Him. It can mean we simply choose not to believe certain aspects about who He is. The bottom line is that unbelief is said to come from an evil heart. We must repent of this and ask the Lord for mercy that we would not doubt Him or stand against who the Word reveals Him to be.

I have noticed through the years that many believe faith is a quiet believing. A religious spirit usually causes this. It pacifies us and makes us think we are doing something spiritual. So often, however, we have just slipped into a melancholy place of unbelief. I try and tell people that faith isn't a quiet believing; it is a violent pursuit. Real faith has a desperateness connected to it. Real faith has an aggressiveness joined to it. Real faith is bold and demanding. It will not let go until it apprehends what it understands belongs to it. Whether it was blind Bartimaeus crying out for his healing, or the woman with the issue of blood, or the lepers calling for Jesus to show them mercy, those who were healed had demonstrative faith. I'm not saying we must do something that is fleshly. I am saying, however, that these people did things in the flesh that manifested the cry and passion that was in their heart. They had a faith that was violent in nature and therefore apprehended their healing. They realized that Jesus, the anointed of God, was in their midst. They could not let this chance pass them by. They took their faith and plugged into the power of the Spirit's presence.

Jesus said something very powerful concerning this in Mark chapter 16, verses 17 and 18. He spoke of the power that would be exhibited through people of faith:

> *And these signs will follow those who believe: In My name they will cast out demons; they will speak with new tongues; they will take up serpents; and if they drink anything deadly, it will by no means hurt them; they will lay hands on the sick, and they will recover.*

Jesus said we would *"lay hands on the sick, and they* [would] *recover"* (Mark 16:18). The laying on of hands is the imparting of the anointing and power of the Holy Spirit. Notice that those who are anointed impart the anointing through their hands. Those who are sick are responsible to recover. The words "they shall recover" in the Greek mean "to get a hold on wellness." So, when the healing anointing is imparted through someone, we must "get a hold on wellness and possess it." This requires faith. We grab hold of that which is being imparted and refuse to let go. This is our plugging into the anointing with our faith and receiving everything it brings to us.

The fourth truth about the Holy Spirit and the anointing is there appears to be two anointings in which Jesus walked. Acts chapter 10 and verse 38 says Jesus walked in the anointing of the Holy Spirit and of power:

> *how God anointed Jesus of Nazareth with the Holy Spirit and with power, who went about doing good and healing all who were oppressed by the devil, for God was with Him.*

Sometimes we just read across this verse and think it is speaking of only the anointing of the Holy Spirit. The truth is, the Holy Spirit is what brings power. Acts chapter 1 and verse 8 clearly states that we receive power when the Holy Spirit comes upon us:

> *But you shall receive power when the Holy Spirit has come upon you; and you shall be witnesses to Me in Jerusalem, and in all Judea and Samaria, and to the end of the earth.*

Even though we do receive power from the Holy Spirit, I also believe there is another dimension we need to see great miracles occur and healing manifested.

In Luke chapter 4 and verse 1, we see Jesus going into the wilderness "filled with the Spirit":

> *Then Jesus, being filled with the Holy Spirit, returned from the Jordan and was led by the Spirit into the wilderness.*

This was a result of His encounter at His baptism in the river Jordan. The heavens opened, the affirming voice of the Father was heard, and the Holy Spirit descended on Him like a dove. He was now sealed and settled in the Father's acceptance and love. In this place, the Spirit of God leads Him into the wilderness. In Luke chapter 4 and verse 14, we see Jesus coming out of the wilderness after forty days. These days have involved temptation by the devil, fasting, and solitude. It appears, however, that something else has transpired while Jesus walked in the wilderness. The Bible says that when Jesus came out of the wilderness, He came out in the "power of the Spirit":

> *Then Jesus returned in the power of the Spirit to Galilee, and news of Him went out through all the surrounding region.*

Jesus went into the wilderness "filled with the Spirit" but comes out in the "power of the Spirit." Connecting this to Acts 10:38, which says He was anointed *"with the Holy Spirit and with power,"* we have to wonder what happened in the wilderness (Acts 10:38). I would submit that Jesus experienced a second anointing. At the river Jordan, the anointing, filling, and baptism of the Holy Spirit came on Him. In the wilderness, He received the anointing of power. It was after this anointing that the signs, wonders, miracles, and healings began to happen. His fame began to spread throughout the region.

I believe there is another dimension of power available to us from the Holy Spirit. It is imperative that we recognize this, or we can live below the level we can access. Paul also spoke of this. First Corinthians chapter 2, verses 4 and 5, tells us that Paul walked in this same dimension:

And my speech and my preaching were not with persuasive words of human wisdom, but in demonstration of the Spirit and of power, that your faith should not be in the wisdom of men but in the power of God.

Paul declared that he functioned in a demonstration of Spirit and of power. I think it is interesting that we are told this is the dimension where men's faith began to be established. Paul recognized the need for our faith not just to be in sound doctrine, but also in the experience of His power.

We also see this in what John the Baptist prophesied about Jesus. He said Jesus would baptize us in the Holy Spirit and fire. Luke chapter 3 and verse 16 declares one of the prophetic purposes of Jesus' coming:

John answered, saying to all, "I indeed baptize you with water; but One mightier than I is coming, whose sandal strap I am not worthy to loose. He will baptize you with the Holy Spirit and fire...."

John promised that Jesus had a baptism of the Holy Spirit *and* of fire. The word *fire* in the Greek is *pur*, and it means "lightning." Lightning is synonymous with power. John G. Lake spoke of the "lightning of God" shooting through his soul. When this occurred, he saw amazing miracles happen. This was a reference to the power of God. All of this tells us there is another dimension and even a second anointing for which we should contend. We should thank God for the anointing of the Holy Spirit that seals us, settles us, affirms us, and grants us revelation of the Fatherhood of God.

However, we must also press for the second anointing in which Jesus and others clearly walked. It is the anointing of power. Perhaps it is just another release and level of the Spirit's ministry through us. However we phrase it, we should desperately desire it. This, it seems, is necessary for the amazing miracles that all desire and many need.

So what allows this "second" anointing? I would suggest that the anointing of the Holy Spirit is a gift. God, from His gracious character, pours this anointing out onto any and all believers who desire Him. I would also suggest that the anointing of power is a "reward" for passing the test of the wilderness. Jesus went into the wilderness "filled." He came out in the "power" of the Spirit, manifesting the Kingdom of God. His filling was a gift. The power was a reward for successfully obeying the Lord in the wilderness through the temptations and trials. We must know that every time we face temptation and trials in a wilderness place, we are being granted the opportunity to qualify for a new place of power! As we embrace the grace of God and overcome, God deems us worthy to carry and function in a new place of power. We can walk in the two anointings—not just the anointing of the Holy Spirit, but also the anointing of power, which people can plug into and receive abundantly from.

The final thought concerning the Holy Spirit and the anointing is that it is a substance. This concept and revelation changed my life. To be able to move in agreement with the Spirit and power, we should know this idea. Sometimes we think the anointing is something mystical. It is spiritual but not necessarily mystical when you understand it. John G. Lake also said, "God is not superstitious. He is scientific." Lake believed the anointing was an actual substance that lived on the inside of us. As a result, it could be transferred, imparted, administered, and used to touch people in need. This idea concerning the anointing comes from an examination of the Scriptures. For instance, the woman with the issue of blood wanted to touch the hem of Jesus' garment. Mark chapter 5, verses 25 through 29, shows this woman's faith and determination. She had her focus on the garment Jesus was wearing.

> Now a certain woman had a flow of blood for twelve years, and had suffered many things from many physicians. She had spent all that she had and was no better, but rather grew worse. When she heard about Jesus, she came behind Him in the crowd and touched His garment. For she said, "If only I may touch His clothes, I shall be made well." Immediately the fountain of her blood was dried up, and she felt in her body that she was healed of the affliction.

Why did she want to touch Jesus' clothes? Some believe there was something religiously special about the garment Jesus wore. I'm not really sure about this. What I do know is that the anointing was in this garment because the anointing on Jesus' life had saturated it. The anointing, being a substance, had permeated the clothes of Jesus. As a result, the woman desired to touch the clothes to pull the anointing out of them. With her faith she made a demand on the anointing that had embedded itself in Jesus' garments. Her focus was on Jesus' clothes because she understood the anointing was a real substance, yet unseen. Again, this is very similar to electricity. We cannot see electricity, yet we know it's a very real substance. It has great power. We have no problem believing it is real because we see the effects of it. The same is true of the anointing. What we carry in our lives and spirits is a very real substance.

We can take the anointing and impart it in many ways. One of the main ways is through the laying on of hands. The laying on of hands is not a symbolic gesture; it is a transference and impartation of the anointing. We take the anointing in our lives and impart it by faith through our hands. This is what Peter did to the lame man at the Beautiful Gate in Acts chapter 3, verses 6 through 8:

> *Then Peter said, "Silver and gold I do not have, but what I do have I give you: In the name of Jesus Christ of Nazareth, rise up and walk." And he took him by the right hand and lifted him up, and immediately his feet and ankle bones received strength. So he, leaping up, stood and walked and entered the temple with them—walking, leaping, and praising God.*

Clearly Peter understood something was in him. There was something he could give to this man that had the power to heal him. Peter took the substance of the anointing that was in him and imparted it to this man. As a result, the man was dramatically healed. The anointing is a very real substance that is the resurrection power of who Jesus is. This power lives in us, and we have the right to impart it as the very substance of God.

This also explains a couple of other occurrences in the Scriptures. Peter used his shadow to heal people. Acts chapter 5, verses 14 and 15, tells the story of Peter's shadow being cast on people and them being healed:

And believers were increasingly added to the Lord, multitudes of both men and women, so that they brought the sick out into the streets and laid them on beds and couches, that at least the shadow of Peter passing by might fall on some of them.

The substance of the anointing on Peter was cast with his shadow on people. As a result, they were healed. This seems magical, yet it is actually a very real phenomenon that is explainable. It was the anointing transmitted by faith into people through Peter's shadow. When you understand the dynamics at work here, it can cause a greater realm of faith to operate. When I began to comprehend this, I started releasing the God who lives in me rather than just petitioning the God in Heaven. This is what the anointing is. It is the God of the universe living on the inside of me. He is manifest in this substance called the anointing that is full of resurrected power. When we know who He is and what is in us, we can release Him and see powerful demonstrations.

This is why Jesus told the disciples that they should go perform supernatural feats and heal the sick. Luke chapter 10, verses 8 and 9, shows us Jesus commissioning them to heal the sick. He didn't tell them to ask God to do it. He told them to take who and what lived inside them and do it themselves.

Whatever city you enter, and they receive you, eat such things as are set before you. And heal the sick there, and say to them, "The kingdom of God has come near to you."

They were to operate in and release the substance that lived in them. They were to then declare, *"The kingdom of God has come near to you"* (Luke 10:9). Healing is a tangible demonstration of the Kingdom manifested. It shows the power of God annihilating the power of satan in a tangible way! This happens because of what lives in us—the very substance of God, called the anointing.

Paul, Peter, and the early Church understood this. This is why certain Scriptures were penned under the inspiration of the Holy Spirit. Colossians chapter 1 and verse 27 declares that Christ lives in us. He is the hope of glory!

> *To them God willed to make known what are the riches of the glory of this mystery among the Gentiles: which is Christ in you, the hope of glory.*

If we knew who and what really lived in us, it would birth a new level of faith from which to operate. When I began to understand the substance of the anointing, my ability to pray in faith skyrocketed. I was no longer asking a God sitting on a throne in Heaven to do something. I was taking the God who is in me and allowing Him to perform supernatural things. This is a major difference. Ephesians chapter 3 and verse 20 speaks of the exceeding abundance of what He can do. It is according to the power working "in us": *"Now to Him who is able to do exceedingly abundantly above all that we ask or think, according to the power that works in us"* (Eph. 3:20).

There are many other Scriptures that speak of Jesus, His power, His faith, and other things living in us. If we could accept by faith that this isn't a spiritual concept alone but also a practical one, things would change dramatically. Remember, "God is not superstitious. He is scientific." We see this again in the story where a man thrown into the tomb of Elisha was raised. Elisha had walked in such an astounding anointing. It had permeated his very being, even his bones. The result, in Second Kings chapter 13, verses 20 and 21, was that a man was resurrected from the dead by touching the anointing-saturated bones of Elisha.

> *Then Elisha died, and they buried him. And the raiding bands from Moab invaded the land in the spring of the year. So it was, as they were burying a man, that suddenly they spied a band of raiders; and they put the man in the tomb of Elisha; and when the man was let down and touched the bones of Elisha, he revived and stood on his feet.*

The substance of the anointing remained in Elisha even after he was dead. There was still such power residing in him that it overcame death and brought a man back to life. This is phenomenal. The only explanation is that the anointing is a substance that can saturate clothes, shadows, hands, words, and even the bones of a dead prophet. May God help us to learn how to administer this anointing that lives in us.

There is one more example of this substance of the anointing operating that I would like to cite. In Acts chapter 19, verses 11 and 12, the Bible says that handkerchiefs were brought from the body of Paul. These "handkerchiefs" were so full of the anointing that Paul carried that they exorcised demons and healed the sick.

> *Now God worked unusual miracles by the hands
> of Paul, so that even handkerchiefs or aprons were
> brought from his body to the sick, and the diseases left
> them and the evil spirits went out of them.*

The word *handkerchiefs* is the Greek word *soudarion*, and it means "a sweat cloth." It refers to a towel for wiping perspiration off the face. Wow! So these were not the pieces of cloth people sell on television to make a profit off of unsuspecting and desperate people. Sorry for the sarcasm. These were literally cloths that Paul wore, potentially while he worked. Perhaps they were what he used to wipe sweat from his face while making tents to support himself and the ministry. Regardless, it is apparent that these "handkerchiefs" were sweat rags brought from his body. This means that the perspiration that flowed from his body carried the anointing of the Spirit. It was so powerful that it healed people and set people free from demons. This occurred because the anointing is a substance.

I do believe it is appropriate to pray over handkerchiefs, cloths, and the like to "impart" the anointing into them. These can then be laid on people, and they can receive miracles from the Lord. The pieces of material actually become storage batteries once the anointing is imparted into them. This is very similar to the batteries used to start our cars. The batteries have no ability to generate power themselves. They can only receive it and hold it until it is needed to crank the car. This is what was happening with these aprons and handkerchiefs. They were able to receive and hold the anointing Paul carried. They could then, by faith, be accessed when they were laid on those in need. When there is a true anointing released into these cloths, the anointing can remain there and bring life to what it touches. This may seem far-fetched to some, but it illustrates the tangibility of the anointing. This is important in getting people healed. It is the substance of the anointing that brings healing to people. This is why many will feel some kind of physical manifestation of fire, heat, electricity, shock, or another demonstration. They are encountering the substance of the anointing.

Yet if there is something legal working to forbid someone from being healed, this legality must be removed. It is possible to experience all sorts of power and demonstrations and still be sick. Only when the legal issue used by the devil is removed can the anointing have its effect. Please remember, though, that sickness and disease are not always a result of something legal against someone. It can be simply the devil moving illegally and working against someone. In this case, we simply take the authority and anointing of the Spirit and administer His life and healing. However, if something legal is allowing it, we must move this out of the way. Once this occurs, the substance of the anointing aggressively received in the Spirit will bring healing. Jesus bought and paid for this. It is our right to receive all things He said were legally ours. The Holy Spirit brings these things to us and allows us the benefits of all Jesus did! Here is a prayer we can pray to operate in the anointing of the Spirit and see people healed:

> *Lord, thank You so much for the anointing of Your Spirit. Lord, help us discern the basis of every demonic activity. We ask to be made aware of whether the devil is moving illegally or legally to afflict with this sickness. Lord, by faith we move in agreement with Your anointing and Spirit. Thank You, Holy Spirit, for*

coming to bring everything Jesus died for into reality in our life. Let any legal thing satan would use now be dissolved and revoked. Holy Spirit, we receive the substance of Your anointing to come and touch all infirmities. We by faith grab hold of the power and presence of the substance of the anointing. We receive that which has the authority to undo all sickness and disease. We shake off all complacency and tolerance of disease. We stir ourselves to embrace Your power, Holy Spirit. In the name of Jesus, we receive the very substance of the anointing that removes and revokes any remaining effect of devilish activity. We receive our healing now from the power of the Spirit. Thank You, Jesus, for all You did to remove the legal rights of the devil. They are broken, and we are now free to receive from Holy Spirit Your full redemption and health. We take it now in Jesus' name. Amen.

CHAPTER 11

PRESENTING OUR CASE FOR HEALING IN THE COURTS

S O OFTEN IT SEEMS THAT I DEAL EXTENSIVELY WITH what the devil is doing legally to stop what Jesus paid for us to have. This is necessary to get things legally in place for breakthrough. We must know how to take the blood of Jesus and remove the case the devil has against us to hold us captive in sickness. Again, Revelation chapter 12, verses 10 and 11, tells us that the accuser is constantly building cases against us:

> *Then I heard a loud voice saying in heaven, "Now salvation, and strength, and the kingdom of our God,*

and the power of His Christ have come, for the accuser of our brethren, who accused them before our God day and night, has been cast down. And they overcame him by the blood of the Lamb and by the word of their testimony, and they did not love their lives to the death.

So, "the accuser of the brethren" is not someone speaking evil or being critical against us in the natural. The accuser that is bringing legal cases against us before God is of demonic origin. We undo these cases by the blood of the Lamb. When we repent, the blood of Jesus is the thing that legally removes and revokes the right of the devil to speak against us. In regard to healing, the legal rights of the devil are annulled and that which the devil is using to hold in sickness is destroyed. It is, however, one thing to have a case against us removed and another thing to make and present a case ourselves. Not only do we overcome the accuser and his case by the blood of the Lamb, we also overcome by "the word of our testimony." This is speaking of our presentation of our case. "The word of our testimony" is the evidence presented that allows God to render verdicts in our favor. This is very powerful and something in which we must learn to walk to secure the healing that Jesus' work on the cross legally provides for us!

The word *testimony* in Revelation chapter 12 and verse 11 is the Greek word *marturia*, and it means "evidence given." It comes from the Greek word *martus*, which means "a judicial witness." So, "the word of our testimony" is when we are presenting evidence before the Throne of God. This allows the Judge to render verdicts. Therefore, not only do we need to undo the case of the accuser against us by the blood of Jesus, but we also must present our own case for healing! If the Court of Heaven is a "real" court, it can only render verdicts based on evidence presented.

Several years ago, I was teaching on the Courts of Heaven in the Chicago, Illinois, area. Even though I was in the United States, I was speaking before a Korean group and was therefore being translated. When I finished one of the sessions, the man hosting the meetings and translating for me shared a story with me. He was a translator in the natural court system of Chicago. When a Korean was in these courts, he was hired to translate into Korean so it was sure that they understood the proceedings. He shared how in a court setting one day, a young attorney was seeking to make his case before the judge. This attorney kept rambling on, seeking to get the necessary facts into evidence. The judge watched, waited, and listened patiently for a good while. Finally, however, the judge interrupted this young attorney. He said, "Young man, please stop." The judge then said to this lawyer, "I know what you're trying to do, but you're going to have to give me a reason." What was he telling this young advocate? The judge was aware of the verdict that was wanted. However, the lawyer had yet to give him evidence that would allow this verdict. He had not made his case. If there is to be a ruling from the court, there must be evidence to substantiate that ruling. Judges can only render verdicts on the basis of the evidence presented. If we are to secure and receive healing from the Courts of Heaven, we must know how to present our case in the courts. If the devil is using something legal to hold someone in sickness, not only do we have to have that legal right revoked, we also need to present "the word of our testimony" to give evidence. This can allow the healing that Jesus bought and paid for to become ours.

There can be many things we can present in the Courts of Heaven as evidence and testimony. The first and foremost thing is what Jesus has done for us. As we approach the courts, we should bring the evidence of the cross. We have discussed previously what Jesus accomplished on the cross. It is appropriate to submit this into evidence in the Courts of Heaven. We can submit before the courts that, according to Isaiah chapter 53 and verse 4, when Jesus died on the cross, He bore away our sickness and carried away our pains:

> *Surely He has borne our griefs and carried our sorrows; yet we esteemed Him stricken, smitten by God, and afflicted.*

We shared previously that the word *griefs* means "maladies, diseases, and sicknesses," while *sorrows* can mean "pains." So, when Jesus died on the cross, He declared sickness illegal. It has lost its legal right to operate against those who belong to Jesus and are in covenant with Him. This is a piece of evidence we should present before the courts.

We can also present the evidence as testimony that Jesus took stripes on Him to secure our healing. Isaiah chapter 53 and verse 5 declares this:

> *But He was wounded for our transgressions, He was bruised for our iniquities; the chastisement for our peace was upon Him, and by His stripes we are healed.*

We can present before the Courts of Heaven that the beating Jesus took was for our healing. We can also present before the courts that after the cross, we are healed already according to First Peter chapter 2 and verse 24:

who Himself bore our sins in His own body on the
tree, that we, having died to sins, might live for righ-
teousness—by whose stripes you were healed.

We take all that Jesus has done for us, and we present it as evidence in the Courts of Heaven. We begin to make our case for healing based on His finished work.

The Holy Spirit will help us as we present our case before the Judge. Remember that the Holy Spirit is the *Parakletos*, which, when searched out, means "a legal aide." This comes from John chapter 14 and verse 16, where the Spirit is called the "Helper":

And I will pray the Father, and He will give you
another Helper, that He may abide with you forever.

This same word is used for Jesus' function in First John chapter 2 and verse 1. We are told that Jesus is our "Advocate":

My little children, these things I write to you, so
that you may not sin. And if anyone sins, we have
an Advocate with the Father, Jesus Christ the
righteous.

The very same word *parakletos* is translated as "helper" but then also as the legal term "advocate." An advocate is some-one who stands in the courts to plead the case of another. Jesus stands to plead our case with us, but the Holy Spirit also empow-ers us and gives us counsel as our legal aide. He helps us know how to make our case and present the evidence. This again is why we are told in Romans chapter 8 and verse 26 that the Spirit helps our weakness. He shows us how to present our case.

> *Likewise the Spirit also helps in our weaknesses. For we do not know what we should pray for as we ought, but the Spirit Himself makes intercession for us with groanings which cannot be uttered.*

The way a case is presented is important to the judge's decisions. We must by faith take any and all things Jesus did for us and present them before the Judge. We are then, by the power of the Spirit, releasing the word of our testimony based on what Jesus has done.

Another thing we should use as testimony is what is written in our book in Heaven. Psalm chapter 139 and verse 16 shows that we have a book in Heaven. In this book is written our destiny and purpose of why we are alive on the earth:

> *Your eyes saw my substance, being yet unformed. And in Your book they all were written, the days fashioned for me, when as yet there were none of them.*

I have shared about this concept at length in my previous books on the Courts of Heaven, particularly about how to access them. Before we ever were alive on the earth, there was a book written about us in Heaven. Our purpose for being alive on the earth is to fulfill that destiny and purpose. When we are presenting our case for healing, it is proper to cite what is written in our book. In other words, we should declare that our healing and health are necessary to fulfill what is in our book.

For instance, one of the main things written in my book is I am called to "disciple nations." I know this because I have heard the Lord clearly tell me so. I need health to be able to do this. So, it would be proper for me to say before the Courts of Heaven, "This is what my mandate is. I cannot fulfill this without a strong body. On the basis of what is written in my book, I am asking for all that Jesus died for me to have to become mine. I ask to be healed. I use what is written in my book as evidence and reasons why healing should be mine." In court, the stronger the case you can make with more evidence, the better.

To present evidence from your book, you need revelation of what is in your book. You need to have an awareness of why you are alive on the earth. Let me give you some ideas of how to discern what is in your book in Heaven so that you can present it as evidence in the courts. First of all, we should cultivate a relationship with the Lord so that we can hear Him. Hearing His voice is critical to discerning what is in your book. John chapter 10 and verse 3 says we are His sheep and therefore should hear His voice:

> *To him the doorkeeper opens, and the sheep hear his voice; and he calls his own sheep by name and leads them out.*

We must pay close attention to the things He has said to us throughout the years. These are very significant clues as to what is in our books. These things we should present before the courts as being in our books. This is why Daniel chapter 7 and verse 10 tells us the court is seated and the books are open:

A fiery stream issued and came forth from before Him. A thousand thousands ministered to Him; ten thousand times ten thousand stood before Him. The court was seated, and the books were opened.

From the books we present evidence into the courts. The things we have heard from the Lord are strategic to our destiny. If sickness is warring against us or threatening to take us out prematurely, we must use what is in our books as evidence and testimony to secure our long life and destiny.

Another clue to what is in you book is found by paying attention to your desires. You will notice that "all my substance yet unformed" was written in the book of Heaven (see Ps. 139:16). This can mean, among other things, my DNA. What makes me tick? What reverberates with me? Whatever is in my book God will have also formed desires consistent with this. I should pay attention to the passions of my heart. They are clues to what is in my book.

My inclinations can also give me insight into what is in my book. What do I gravitate toward? What kind of people do I enjoy? If I let "nature take its course," where do I end up? These can be signs of what is in my book.

I should also pay attention to my mixture of gifts. Whatever I am gifted in will be consistent with what is in my book. God didn't give me gifts contrary to what is in my book. I am good at specific things because they are necessary to fulfill what is written about me in Heaven.

A final thing to consider concerning what is in our book in Heaven is where my frustrations lie. My frustrations exist because

I was created to solve those problems. That is why they are so frustrating. Our frustrations can be a real sign of what is written in our book. The Holy Spirit will help us discern what is the destiny written in our book. We can then present from our book evidence into the Courts of Heaven. If sickness is seeking to thwart what is in our book, we can petition the court to have it removed. God wants us healed and delivered to be able to fulfill what is in our book in Heaven.

Another part of "the word of our testimony" and evidence we should present is the promises in God's Word. There are promises God gives us as His children. There are promises also connected to our faith and obedience. We should present these as evidence before the Courts of Heaven. Psalm chapter 91, verses 1 through 16, is filled with promises of healing, health, wholeness, and protection. We are told that if we abide in the secret place and make the Lord our refuge, we are preserved.

> *He who dwells in the secret place of the Most High shall abide under the shadow of the Almighty. I will say of the Lord, "He is my refuge and my fortress; my God, in Him I will trust." Surely He shall deliver you from the snare of the fowler and from the perilous pestilence. He shall cover you with His feathers, and under His wings you shall take refuge; His truth shall be your shield and buckler. You shall not be afraid of the terror by night, nor of the arrow that flies by day, nor of the pestilence that walks in darkness, nor of the destruction that lays waste at noonday. A thousand may fall at your side, and ten thousand at your right*

hand; but it shall not come near you. Only with your eyes shall you look, and see the reward of the wicked. Because you have made the Lord, who is my refuge, even the Most High, your dwelling place, no evil shall befall you, nor shall any plague come near your dwelling; for He shall give His angels charge over you, to keep you in all your ways. In their hands they shall bear you up, lest you dash your foot against a stone. You shall tread upon the lion and the cobra, the young lion and the serpent you shall trample underfoot. "Because he has set his love upon Me, therefore I will deliver him; I will set him on high, because he has known My name. He shall call upon Me, and I will answer him; I will be with him in trouble; I will deliver him and honor him. With long life I will satisfy him, and show him My salvation."

It would be appropriate to submit this as evidence in the Courts of Heaven. The promises of God concerning healing contained in this psalm are powerful. He delivers us from *"perilous pestilence"* (Ps. 91:3). He saves us from *"pestilence that walks in darkness"* and *"destruction that lays waste at noonday"* (Ps. 91:6). There are diseases that cause people to "waste away." God delivers us from them. Even though thousands fall around us, it will not touch us (see Ps. 91:7). We will not become a statistic. We can present this in the courts as evidence from God's Word! What touches others will not touch us. Only with our eyes will we behold the reward of the wicked (see Ps. 91:8). God promises divine health and protection. No plague will touch our dwelling or those in our house. The angels will cover us and keep us from all of this (see Ps.

91:10-11). We will not even dash our foot on a stone. The angels of God will carry us in their hands (see Ps. 91:12). With a long and satisfying life will we see His salvation (see Ps. 91:16)! These are promises of God's Word that we should present in the Courts of Heaven. This is evidence the courts love to hear from the faith of God's people.

There are also very distinct promises of healing made to those who do certain things. In Isaiah chapter 58, verses 6 through 8, we see God promising health that breaks forth quickly:

> *Is this not the fast that I have chosen: to loose the bonds of wickedness, to undo the heavy burdens, to let the oppressed go free, and that you break every yoke? Is it not to share your bread with the hungry, and that you bring to your house the poor who are cast out; when you see the naked, that you cover him, and not hide yourself from your own flesh? Then your light shall break forth like the morning, your healing shall spring forth speedily, and your righteousness shall go before you; the glory of the Lord shall be your rear guard.*

God promises that if we minister to others in their need and desperation, our healing can break forth speedily. If we have ministered to others, fed the hungry, taken care of the poor, and clothed the naked, God promises divine health. We can take this and present it as evidence in the Courts of Heaven before a just God. Based on His justice, He can then render a verdict of healing and health. Psalm chapter 41, verses 1 through 3, says what the Lord will do to those who care for the poor:

> *Blessed is he who considers the poor; the Lord will deliver him in time of trouble. The Lord will preserve him and keep him alive, and he will be blessed on the earth; you will not deliver him to the will of his enemies. The Lord will strengthen him on his bed of illness; you will sustain him on his sickbed.*

God promises healing when someone has cared for the poor. We can take this promise if we have done this and present it as evidence before the Lord.

I remember getting a prayer request for healing for a certain well-known ministry. They were having a very serious surgery, and the outcome was questionable. This one was advanced in age and had other things complicating the procedure. As I began to lift them before the Lord, I heard to Lord say to present Psalm 41:1-3 before the courts on their behalf. I knew the Lord said they had cared for the poor and the distressed. I asked before the courts that they would be healed on the basis of this promise. I presented it as evidence before the courts. The report came back very quickly that the surgery they had was a success and they were well and healed. Their ministry before the Lord to the poor was received as testimony. Learning to present the promises of God before the Lord as evidence can produce great results.

It is appropriate to present evidence of our walk with the Lord before the courts. For instance, Proverbs chapter 3, verses 7 and 8, reveals the power of the fear of the Lord:

> *Do not be wise in your own eyes; fear the Lord and depart from evil. It will be health to your flesh, and strength to your bones.*

We can come before His courts and humbly testify that we have sought to depart from evil and fear the Lord. Therefore, on the basis of this testimony, we ask for health to our flesh and strength to our bones.

We can also present before the courts our case that we have paid attention to and reverenced His Word. Proverbs chapter 4, verses 20 through 22, gives the promise of life and health to the flesh of those who obediently listen to the Word of God and let it direct their lives:

> *My son, give attention to my words; incline your ear to my sayings. Do not let them depart from your eyes; keep them in the midst of your heart; for they are life to those who find them, and health to all their flesh.*

We can humbly present the evidence of our life and ask to be forgiven in any and every place in which we haven't been faithful. We can also say that through the power of the Holy Spirit, we have sought to order our lives as best we can according to the Word of God. We can ask for healing from the courts on the basis of this testimony. We should always be humble before the courts of Heaven but not ashamed to present evidence of our efforts to obey Him. There are books in Heaven that have recorded everything about us. So, when we present our testimony, these books will be consulted to verify our evidence. If it is found to be true, there can be verdicts rendered as a result. I believe Malachi spoke of some of these books in Malachi chapter 3 and verse 16. They are called Books of Remembrance, and they cause us to be remembered before the Lord.

*Then those who feared the Lord spoke to one another,
and the Lord listened and heard them; so a book of
remembrance was written before Him for those who
fear the Lord and who meditate on His name*

These books can testify of us in the courts and cause us to
be remembered. They can verify our obedience and heart for the
Lord and cause us to be remembered. It is proper to ask for these
books to speak and verify our history with God.

There is one more piece of evidence that we should present
before the courts that I will mention in this chapter. We should
present the mercy of God as evidence. In Mark chapter 10 and
verse 47, we see a man called blind Bartimaeus crying out to Jesus
and asking for mercy:

*And when he heard that it was Jesus of Nazareth, he
began to cry out and say, "Jesus, Son of David, have
mercy on me!"*

We know that Jesus did stop to heal this man. Bartimaeus's
cry was on the basis of mercy. Many others in the New Testament
asked Jesus for mercy as they were healed. When we approach the
Courts of Heaven, we should come in the midst of every other testimony, releasing the evidence of His mercy. We can declare that
"God, You are merciful. I am asking for healing on the basis of
Your kind and merciful nature. In the midst of all the other evidence I have presented, I am only worthy to be healed by You
because of what You have done and because of the mercy it has
released." This, I believe, speaks boldly before the Courts of
Heaven. Presenting evidence and releasing our word of testimony

is critical to approaching the courts. God's desire is to heal. He has given us the privilege of petitioning His court for it. In the next chapter, I will give us one more piece of evidence we should present in the courts for healing. Here is a prayer you can pray based on the evidence we have talked about in this chapter:

> *Lord, we present before Your courts all that Jesus, Your Son, has done. We thank You for Your work on my behalf on the cross. Lord, we thank You for everything You suffered. Thank You for the beating You took for our healing. Thank You for hanging on the cross, carrying away our sickness, and bearing away our pain. Thank You for the stripes on Your back. We can never say thank You enough. We now present all You did on the cross on my behalf before Your courts. Let it now speak for me in the Courts of Heaven. We receive our healing on the basis of Your cross!*
>
> *Lord, we also bring before Your courts all that You have written in our book of destiny. I thank You that we have a book written in Heaven about us and our future and purpose. Lord, we need health and wholeness to fulfill what is in our book. We present before You all that is in our book. We ask before this court that healing and power will flow into our bodies that we might complete what is in our book. We thank You for a long and satisfying life that we may accomplish all that is written about us. We have come, O God, to do Your will!*
>
> *Lord, we come before Your courts based on the promise of Your Word. Thank You for the grace You give us*

to obey You. Thanks so much for the promises of Your Word. We bring Your Word and promises before Your courts and present them as evidence. They are the word of our testimony. They declare Your faithfulness and kindness to us. Lord, we remind this court that Psalm 91 declares freedom from sickness, pestilence, plagues, injury, and hurts. We present Your Word and ask that all that it promises in Psalm 91 would be ours. We ask before this court that angels bear us up in their hands and that You satisfy us with a long life. We also petition this court that all ministry to the poor would be recognized by this court. We ask according to Your Word that we would be made whole from all sickness and that healing would flow to us. May all we have done for the poor and all that is recorded in books in Heaven be brought to the courts and verified. Let it speak on our behalf before this court. We also submit to this court that we have sought to walk in the fear of the Lord and to depart from evil. We have not always fully obeyed in this, however. We ask for forgiveness concerning this. We ask, though, that according to Your Word, it would be health to our flesh. Let our history of obedience speak before Your court. Also, we have made Your Word our food. We ask that our love for Your Word would speak in this court as well and allow health to our flesh to now come. We also ask and petition this court that Your mercy would speak for us. Lord, thank You for Your mercy. We remind this court that when You, Lord Jesus, walked the earth, You healed on the basis of mercy. Would You now allow Your mercy to flow to us? Lord, we ask from this court for the healing that Jesus died for us to have. Thank You so much for the healing and life that is flowing to us. In Jesus' name. Amen.

CHAPTER 12

PRESENTING MORE EVIDENCE FOR HEALING

WE HAVE DEALT WITH SEVERAL PIECES OF EVIDENCE that can be presented as "the word of our testimony." In this chapter, I want to deal with one more that I believe carries great weight before the Courts of Heaven. Those who will build God a house secure for themselves healing. When the Jewish leaders approached Jesus concerning a centurion who had sickness in his house, Jesus responded and went with them to bring healing. The facts given to Jesus concerning this activity moved Him to go to this Gentile's house. The principle is that when this evidence is presented and the testimony given, it can securing healing.

In Luke chapter 7, verses 1 through 10, we see this story of a Roman centurion with a sick servant who is about to die. Jesus is petitioned by the elders of the Jews to help this man and heal his servant.

Now when He concluded all His sayings in the hearing of the people, He entered Capernaum. And a certain centurion's servant, who was dear to him, was sick and ready to die. So when he heard about Jesus, he sent elders of the Jews to Him, pleading with Him to come and heal his servant. And when they came to Jesus, they begged Him earnestly, saying that the one for whom He should do this was deserving, "for he loves our nation, and has built us a synagogue."

Then Jesus went with them. And when He was already not far from the house, the centurion sent friends to Him, saying to Him, "Lord, do not trouble Yourself, for I am not worthy that You should enter under my roof. Therefore I did not even think myself worthy to come to You. But say the word, and my servant will be healed. For I also am a man placed under authority, having soldiers under me. And I say to one, 'Go,' and he goes; and to another, 'Come,' and he comes; and to my servant, 'Do this,' and he does it." When Jesus heard these things, He marveled at him, and turned around and said to the crowd that followed Him, "I say to you, I have not found such great faith, not even in Israel!" And those who were

*sent, returning to the house, found the servant well
who had been sick.*

There are powerful truths in this story that show the things
that move the heart of God. We can see from this story how to
potentially present a case for healing in the Courts of Heaven.
This centurion was Roman, which made him disqualified from
receiving from the Lord at this present time. Remember that
during Jesus' earthly ministry, He was sent only to the House of
Israel. This meant that healing, deliverance, and the touch of God
through Jesus was only for the Jews. It would not be until after
the cross that the Gentiles would be brought into the covenant.
This is why Jesus said He was only sent to the Jews. Matthew chapter 15 and verse 24 shows Jesus declaring this as a Gentile woman
pleaded for healing for her daughter:

> *But He answered and said, "I was not sent except to
> the lost sheep of the house of Israel."*

Jesus did heal her daughter because of her persistent faith. She
was able to reach into that which was yet to come and pull it into
the now. This is the power of faith. The only other time I see in
Scripture where Jesus ministered to a non-Jew was here with this
centurion. What was it that caused Jesus to go with the elders of
the Jews and minister healing to someone in this Roman's house?
It was two things that they used to plead their case before Jesus.
They told Jesus, "He loves our nation, and he has built us a synagogue." When Jesus heard these two things, He was moved to
go with them. Healing was indeed secured for this man's house.
The servant who was about to die was healed and made well. The

reason Jesus agreed to do this for this man was his heart for Israel and his building of God's house!

We are aware that God promised a blessing for all who love Israel. God's promise to Abraham is found in Genesis chapter 12, verses 1 through 3:

> *Now the Lord had said to Abram: "Get out of your country, from your family and from your father's house, to a land that I will show you. I will make you a great nation; I will bless you and make your name great; and you shall be a blessing. I will bless those who bless you, and I will curse him who curses you; and in you all the families of the earth shall be blessed."*

God promised to bless all who bless Israel. He also said there would be a curse on those who cursed this God-chosen nation. This is God's promise to Abraham and a part of the Abrahamic covenant. This is why Jesus agreed to go and heal the man in this centurion's house. The plea based on the man's love of Israel allowed this. We too can petition the Courts of Heaven based on our love and heart for Israel. This carries great influence and weight before the Courts of Heaven. It is appropriate to state our case, including a heart and desire toward God's people. He will bless those who bless Israel.

The second thing that they used to petition Jesus was this man's building of a synagogue. He, as a Roman soldier, had built God a house! When someone builds God a house, it gives that person standing and position in the spirit realm. I believe it gives them a place to present cases in the Courts of Heaven. It becomes a piece of the evidence that can speak on their behalf.

This is especially true when we are in need of healing. When this Roman soldier built the house of God, it caused Heaven to give him a place from which petitions could be made. Anyone who builds God a house or involves themselves in building God a house is esteemed before Heaven. Whether we do this through hands-on involvement, donations, serving in the house, or contributing in other capacities, it can give us a place from which we can petition God. Especially when it comes to asking God for healing to flow into our house, those who have built God a house have this place.

We see this in particular portions of Scripture. When the Shunammite woman and her husband built a room for the prophet Elisha to live in, her barrenness was healed. Second Kings chapter 4, verses 15 through 17, shows Elisha speaking the word to the woman from the room she had built for him:

> *So he said, "Call her." When he had called her, she stood in the doorway. Then he said, "About this time next year you shall embrace a son." And she said, "No, my lord. Man of God, do not lie to your maidservant!" But the woman conceived, and bore a son when the appointed time had come, of which Elisha had told her.*

This woman and her husband built a room for the one who represented God to them. She was in fact building God a house. The result was a word spoken that broke barrenness and built her house! When we build God a house, He will build our house! This is exactly what happened to the centurion. He built God a house, and Jesus released healing into his house and built it. Sickness was trying to destroy it, but because of what he had done, it was sustained and built.

We also see this principle in Exodus chapter 1, verses 20 and 21. Pharaoh commanded the midwives who helped in the birthing process to kill the male children. He was afraid of the prophesied leader arising to deliver Israel. The midwives, however, feared God and wouldn't do it. The Bible speaks of the blessing that came on them because they built the house of Israel rather than destroying it:

> *Therefore God dealt well with the midwives, and the people multiplied and grew very mighty. And so it was, because the midwives feared God, that He provided households for them.*

When the midwives brought life instead of death and built God's house by blessing the people of Israel, God gave them households. In other words, they had families themselves. The principle is clear: when we build God a house, He builds our house.

We can also see this principle in the Book of Haggai where the people put their own houses ahead of the house of God and it resulted in negative things happening to their house. Haggai chapter 1, verses 3 through 9, shows the Lord's displeasure because the people were building their own houses rather than the house of God:

> *Then the word of the Lord came by Haggai the prophet, saying, "Is it time for you yourselves to dwell in your paneled houses, and this temple to lie in ruins?" Now therefore, thus says the Lord of hosts: "Consider your ways! You have sown much, and bring*

> *in little; you eat, but do not have enough; you drink,*
> *but you are not filled with drink; you clothe your-*
> *selves, but no one is warm; and he who earns wages,*
> *earns wages to put into a bag with holes." Thus says*
> *the Lord of hosts: "Consider your ways! Go up to the*
> *mountains and bring wood and build the temple, that*
> *I may take pleasure in it and be glorified," says the*
> *Lord. "You looked for much, but indeed it came to*
> *little; and when you brought it home, I blew it away.*
> *Why?" says the Lord of hosts. "Because of My house*
> *that is in ruins, while every one of you runs to his own*
> *house.*

Their houses were not being blessed and actually were being resisted because they were *not* building God's house.

The encouraging thing is that the moment they corrected this, things shifted in the spirit and the blessing returned. Haggai chapter 2, verses 18 and 19, shows how the moment they began to build, a shift in the spirit realm caused the blessing to be released:

> *Consider now from this day forward, from the twen-*
> *ty-fourth day of the ninth month, from the day that*
> *the foundation of the Lord's temple was laid—*
> *consider it: Is the seed still in the barn? As yet the vine,*
> *the fig tree, the pomegranate, and the olive tree have*
> *not yielded fruit. But from this day I will bless you.*

Even though things didn't look different in the natural, the prophet declared that things had moved in the spirit because the people had begun to build the house. It was only a matter of time until the fruitfulness returned. Their building of God's house had secured blessings and fruitfulness back to their lives—and even to the nation. We could look at many other examples connected to building God a house. The truth is, this action gives us a place from which we can petition the Courts of Heaven. This is why Jesus responded to the request to go and heal the servant in the centurion's house. To be involved in building God a house can position us to petition the court for healing.

When I speak of building God a house, it can be our involvement in a local church. However, it is not limited to just this. Perhaps God has placed it in your heart to help expand His work through other forms. Maybe your support and effort in missions would qualify? Or maybe supporting and helping a prayer ministry in a nation or for a nation? Perhaps it is helping see the apostolic move of God shift the culture of a nation? Maybe it is being a part of an apostolic family whose heart and efforts are directed toward seeing nations fulfill their divine destiny? Building God's house can be a multifaceted effort. I am stating this because if you have been involved in some of these or other things, it could give you the right to petition the Courts of Heaven for healing.

This is what happened with the centurion. When Jesus was almost to his house, a friend came to meet Him. He communicated that the soldier didn't feel worthy to stand before Jesus; neither did he esteem himself worthy for Jesus to enter his house. The friend then said the words that amazed Jesus. He said the centurion wanted Jesus to only speak the word and his servant that was sick would be healed. Jesus was amazed. Here was a Gentile who understood a mystery of the spirit realm. He understood the power and mystery of alignment and as a result was operating in great faith! The centurion shared that he was a man under the authority of the Roman government. Therefore, he had authority himself. His words, as a result, carried power. He could tell people to do things, and they did it because the authority he carried derived from his alignment with Rome. The centurion was declaring that he understood the same thing about Jesus: Jesus carried authority because of His perfect alignment with the government of Heaven. Therefore, just like the centurion's words caused things to move in the natural realm, Jesus' words moved things in the spirit realm! All He had to do was speak the word, and healing would flow into his house! This is exactly what happened. They returned to the house and found the servant completely healed. The words of Jesus from a distance had released healing into this man's house. However, the driving thing that allowed the words of Jesus to have their effect was the building of God's house. It was the evidence presented that brought Jesus to his house in the first place.

We should learn how to present our case for healing in our house based on our honoring of and love for Israel and our history of building God a house. This is a prayer and evidence we can bring into the courts. Our word of testimony can be used to present our case. Here is an example of a prayer that we might bring to the Courts of Heaven as we submit our case for healing:

> *Lord, I approach Your courts now. I thank You that the blood of Jesus silences any case against me. Anything that would resist my healing is revoked and removed. I acknowledge and know that You purchased healing for me on Your cross. When You were*

brutally afflicted and died, You carried away sickness and disease and bore away my pains. I thank You for all You have done for me. I now come before You, Lord, as Judge of all. I acknowledge all the voices that are speaking on my behalf before this court. I want to ask that all Jesus died for concerning my healing would now flow into my house. As evidence before this court I want to declare my love for Your people Israel. Your Word clearly declares that You will bless whomever blesses them. I love Your people Israel and state before this court that they are Your covenant people. I ask for the blessing of God to come over them and for all You intended for them to become a reality.

I further state before this court that I have involved myself in the building of Your house. Even as the centurion built Your house and it moved You to release healing into his house, I ask for Your healing in my house. I ask that sickness and disease would be taken from the midst of my house (see Exod. 23:25). Lord, I love Your house. I have sought with my efforts, my finances, my service, and my loyalty to build Your house. I now ask, because I seek to build Your house, that You would build my house. I ask, even as the centurion's house received healing because he built Your house, let healing flow into my house, Lord! I ask that every form of sickness that would seek to tear down my house now be judged from Your courts. I ask that sickness and disease be removed and healing and wholeness be restored. Lord, thank You for rendering a verdict of judgment against this sickness from Your courts. In Your vengeance from Your throne now let this sickness be declared illegal and unrighteous and its power broken. I receive from Your courts the healing virtue of the Lord into my life. Thank You, Lord, so much!

CHAPTER 13

LAYING OUR LIVES DOWN

WHEN WE SEEK TO SILENCE THE ACCUSER SPOKEN OF IN Revelation chapter 12, verses 10 and 11, we use the blood and the word of our testimony, but we also must lay our lives down. This is the posture from which we approach the Courts of Heaven. Even when approaching the courts for healing, laying our lives down must be a part of the procedure.

> *Then I heard a loud voice saying in heaven, "Now salvation, and strength, and the kingdom of our God, and the power of His Christ have come, for the accuser of our brethren, who accused them before our God day and night, has been cast down. And they overcame*

him by the blood of the Lamb and by the word of
their testimony, and they did not love their lives to the
death...."

The willingness and ability to lay our lives down to death grants us great authority, influence, and place in the Courts of Heaven to present our case. Laying our lives down is not about just giving up our natural, physical lives. There are definitely those who have done so for Jesus. These have a great reward. "Not loving our lives unto death" also speaks of laying down our own preferences, desires, comforts, and conveniences to serve the Lord. The word *lives* in the Greek in this Scripture is *suche*, and the idea is our soulish life. In other words, I sacrifice that which I would prefer and choose. When I willingly do this, I am not loving my life unto death.

When Mary and Martha came to Jesus after the death of Lazarus they both spoke the same words to Jesus. We see this in John chapter 11, verses 21 and 32. In verse 21, Martha speaks from her heart of pain:

Now Martha said to Jesus, "Lord, if You had been
here, my brother would not have died."

The grief in her heart caused her to speak an accusation against the Lord. She was saying, "It's Your fault, Lord. You could have stopped this. Where were You? We called for You. Why didn't You come? Lord, if You had been here, this wouldn't have happened." Martha is possibly spewing allegations against the Lord from a life that hadn't been laid down.

Mary, on the other hand, is one who has cultivated a life surrendered in the deepest recesses of her heart. She speaks the same words as Martha, but from a completely different spirit. In verse 32, we see her coming to Jesus. Instead of an accusation from a not-surrendered heart, she, with the same words as Martha, declares a statement of faith:

> *Then, when Mary came where Jesus was, and saw Him, she fell down at His feet, saying to Him, "Lord, if You had been here, my brother would not have died."*

Mary falls down at the feet of Jesus. She lays her life down and speaks from this place of surrender. Her statement is not only a statement of faith, but also a declaration of worship. She is saying, "I know who You are. I know the power You have. I don't understand why this has happened. Yet I trust You." The result of this interaction was Jesus said, "Where have you laid him?" Jesus is now about to perform one of His most powerful miracles. I believe there was something in Mary's yielded heart and willingness to lay her life down that moved Jesus. I am aware that this was the plan all along. Jesus purposely allowed Lazarus to die. This was so He could manifest His glory in this situation. Yet clearly Jesus was moved by the surrender and yielded place of Mary's heart. Her tears of love and adoration mixed with her grief moved His heart. The laying down of her life had great power before the Lord. We must know that our ability to come to this place of surrender carries great power in the Courts of Heaven. Prayers and petitions presented in the courts from a broken and humble heart move the Courts of Heaven. Requests made out of this place carry great weight.

From this encounter with Mary, Jesus goes to the tomb of Lazarus. He raises Lazarus from the dead. We should, however, be aware of the *way* He did this. Knowing the "ways" of God is very important. Psalm chapter 103 and verse 7 says Moses knew God's ways:

> *He made known His ways to Moses, His acts to the children of Israel.*

The children of Israel only experienced what God did. Moses understood how God did it and what caused it to work. When we know only the acts, they cannot necessarily be duplicated. However, when we know His ways, we can reproduce the results over and over again.

We can discover a very significant "way" that God does things in this story of Lazarus's resurrection. Notice that Jesus declares that He has been praying over the days of Lazarus's sickness, death, and burial. He hasn't been idle in the spirit realm. Jesus has been very active, preparing in the spirit what was necessary for the miracle about to happen. He says in John chapter 11, verses 41 and 42, that He has been praying leading up to this moment:

> *Then they took away the stone from the place where the dead man was lying. And Jesus lifted up His eyes and said, "Father, I thank You that You have heard Me. And I know that You always hear Me, but because of the people who are standing by I said this, that they may believe that You sent Me."*

Jesus had clearly been praying. Why would Jesus be investing times of prayer over this situation? I want to propose to you that He was dealing with every legal thing that had allowed Lazarus to die prematurely. Even though God allowed it, Lazarus's death was caused by the devil. The devil cannot do anything except he has discovered a legal right to do it. This is especially true in premature death. Jesus understood that before He could raise Lazarus, the legal right used to kill him prematurely had to be revoked. Jesus had undone this through His prayers. Perhaps it was Lazarus's own sin or transgression. I would think, though, that it was probably connected to something in Lazarus's bloodline that had given the devil the legal right to take him out. Jesus, through His prayers, had dealt with the bloodline issues in Lazarus. Perhaps He had undone any legal claim of the devil to own Lazarus that allowed a case against Lazarus in the spirit realm. Whatever it was, Jesus, through prayer, had peeled away the legal case of the devil.

When He stepped to the mouth of this tomb, He had no need to pray more. Now He could make a decree of authority and power, and resurrection life was free to raise Lazarus. We see this in John chapter 11, verses 43 and 44:

> *Now when He had said these things, He cried with a loud voice, "Lazarus, come forth!" And he who had died came out bound hand and foot with graveclothes, and his face was wrapped with a cloth. Jesus said to them, "Loose him, and let him go."*

Lazarus was raised from the dead because Jesus, through prayer, had undone all the legalities the devil used. Once this was done, the life and power of the Lord were free to bring life, healing, and resurrection.

There is resurrection life available to us. Jesus is the Healer. There are definitely legal things satan uses to hold people in sickness and even cause many to die prematurely. Whether it is for family members, the multitudes, or ourselves, we can approach the throne of His courts. The Lord has granted us the right to step into the third dimension of prayer and remove every legal issue. As we do, we will see many powerful miracles occur. Just as Jesus did in response to the cry of Mary from a laid-down life, so Heaven's court will respond to us. Here is a prayer to lay down our life before the court and make our petition:

> *Lord, I come before Your courts. As I come approaching Your throne, I lay my life down. I receive Your grace to surrender every part to You. I ask to be broken before You as a vessel of the Lord. Even as Mary fell at Your feet, I fall before You in my spirit. I yield myself before You. I ask that every place of accusation, anger, and any sense of injustice I feel toward You be removed from me. Take every aspect of the Martha spirit out of me. Help me to deal with my pain before You. Even as Mary, I acknowledge and trust You. Forgive me for any place I would blame You on any level. I surrender my "suche" life before You. I now ask from this place of surrender before Your courts that healing would flow. I ask that the very resurrection life of God would move in this realm of sickness. Lord, thank You for all You have done. I now, from this place of surrender, receive from the fullness of the cross. I command from Your courts sickness to be broken and healing received! In Jesus' name. Amen.*

Come before His courts! Healing awaits you!

ABOUT
ROBERT HENDERSON

ROBERT HENDERSON IS A GLOBAL APOSTOLIC LEADER who operates in revelation and impartation. His teaching empowers the body of Christ to see the hidden truths of Scripture clearly and apply them for breakthrough results. Driven by a mandate to disciple nations through writing and speaking, Robert travels extensively around the globe, teaching on the apostolic, the Kingdom of God, the "Seven Mountains," and, most notably, the Courts of Heaven. He has been married to Mary for forty years. They have six children and five grandchildren. Together they are enjoying life in beautiful Midlothian, TX.

For the full *Receiving Healing from the Courts of Heaven Curriculum* and more from Robert Henderson, visit www.roberthenderson.org/store

INCREASE THE EFFECTIVENESS OF YOUR PRAYERS.

Learn how to release your destiny from Heaven's Courts!

Unlocking Destinies from the Courts of Heaven
Curriculum Box Set Includes:
9 Video Teaching Sessions (2 DVD Disks), Unlocking Destinies *book,*
Interactive Manual, Leader's Guide

here are books in Heaven that record your destiny and purpose. Their pages escribe the very reason you were placed on the Earth.

nd yet, there is a war against your destiny being fulfilled. Your archenemy, the evil, knows that as you occupy your divine assignment, by default, the powers darkness are demolished. Heaven comes to Earth as God's people fulfill their ingdom callings!

the *Unlocking Destinies from the Courts of Heaven* book and curriculum, Robert enderson takes you step by step through a prophetic prayer strategy. By atching the powerful video sessions and going through the Courts of Heaven ocess using the interactive manual, you will learn how to dissolve the delays d hindrances to your destiny being fulfilled.